THE LIVING MESSAGE OF ISAIAH

THE LIVING MESSAGE OF ISAIAH

L. LA MAR ADAMS

Deseret Book Company
Salt Lake City, Utah
1981

Library of Congress Cataloging in Publication Data

Adams, L. La Mar, 1934-
  The living message of Isaiah.

  Bibliography: p.
  Includes index.
  1. Bible. O.T. Isaiah—Criticism, interpretation,
etc. I. Title.
BS1515.2.A3   224'.106   81-9816
ISBN 0-87747-875-9   AACR2

Contents

Preface

The purpose of this book is to help us appreciate and understand Isaiah, and to encourage us to keep the Savior's commandment to diligently study the prophecies of Isaiah. Prayerful and humble study of the words of Isaiah will bring us closer to the Savior. Seeking the Spirit, using the spirit of revelation, and inquiring of the Lord concerning Isaiah's prophecies will help us develop great faith in the Lord. Studying the book of Isaiah will result in a tremendous love for Isaiah's words, for the prophet Isaiah, and most of all, for the Savior.

A few Latter-day Saints have expressed the idea that the General Authorities of the Church live and talk the way they do because they are General Authorities, and that Church standards are idealistic and not practical for everyday life. However, if we are to go where Isaiah is, we will need to know what Isaiah knows. We will need to become like Isaiah and the other prophets, for they became like the Savior, and we must become one with them in the Lord if we are to become joint heirs with them.

We are living in a day of the fulfillment of the prophecies of Isaiah. The more we read his words, the more we understand of our own day and the more confidence we have, even in this day of confusion.

Each time we read the words of Isaiah, we are changed. The more we read, the happier is our state, the more exceeding is our joy, the more like Christ we become. Nephi said, "And we talk of Christ, we rejoice in Christ, we preach of Christ, we prophesy of Christ, and we write according to our prophecies, that our children may know to what source they may look for a remission of their sins." (2 Ne. 25:26.)

He who thinks about Christ, speaks about Christ, and acts like Christ, will in the end become like Christ. That is, the more we think of Christ the more we will experience him in our personal lives. Each week during the sacrament we covenant to "always remember him, that [we] may have his Spirit" with us. (D&C 20:79.) The more we diligently study the words of Isaiah and seek to obtain his promises, the closer we can expect to become to the Savior.

(Note: "HC" refers to Joseph Smith's *History of the Church.* *"Teachings"* refers to *Teachings of the Prophet Joseph Smith.* In some instances, scriptures quoted have been revised by the author to more fully agree with the sense of the original languages.)

Acknowledgments

I deeply appreciate my lovely wife, Sandra, who helped transform my work into something more acceptable.

I also appreciate Trevor and Clover Christensen and other friends and relatives who encouraged me to "put it in a book" after hearing my lectures on Isaiah.

1
Of Great Worth Are the Words of Isaiah

In the past several years, interest in the book of Isaiah has soared to new heights among the Saints, both youth and adults. One reason for this increased interest is the admonitions of both Nephi and the Savior to study Isaiah.

Does My Salvation Depend on It?
Nephi declared that the prophecies of Isaiah "are of worth unto the children of men." It appears as though Nephi could hear us inquiring, "But how can they be of great worth when we can't even understand them?"; for Nephi added, "... and he that supposeth that they are not, unto them will I speak particularly ... for I know that they shall be of great worth unto them in the last days." (2 Ne. 25:8.)

Nearly six hundred years later, the Savior himself confirmed Nephi's statement when He told the Nephites, "Great are the words of Isaiah." In fact, the words of Isaiah are so important to us that the Savior made it a commandment to study them: "Yea, a commandment I give unto you that ye search these things diligently." (3 Ne. 23:1.) Since our exaltation depends on our keeping all of the Savior's commandments, searching the words of Isaiah diligently may have something to do with our salvation.

Elder Bruce R. McConkie of the Council of the Twelve queried: "If our eternal salvation depends upon our ability to understand the writings of Isaiah ... how shall we fare in that great day when ... we shall stand before ... Him who said: 'Great are the words of Isaiah'? (3 Ne. 23:1.)" Elder McConkie then suggested: "It just may be that my salvation (and yours also!) does in fact depend upon

1

our ability to understand the writings of Isaiah as fully and truly as Nephi understood them." (*Ensign*, Oct. 1973, p. 78.)

Can Isaiah Be Understood?

While reading the Book of Mormon four or five times as a teenager, I gained a great love, as many have, for the prophet Nephi. Each time through the Book of Mormon, I would read these words: "I, Nephi, write more of the words of Isaiah, for my soul delighteth in his words." (2 Ne. 11:2.) After reading these words, I felt estranged. My mind would turn to Nephi's statement that the words of Isaiah "are plain unto all those that are filled with the spirit of prophecy." (2 Ne. 25:4.) I would think, "I must not be filled with the spirit of prophecy, for I do not understand Isaiah's words."

This, however, was the wrong conclusion. The truth was that I did not apply the spirit of prophecy to the words of Isaiah. Instead, I would skip over them, or at least rush through them, when reading the Book of Mormon. If I had applied the spirit of prophecy by studying it out in my own mind and then asking the Lord, I would have been greatly rewarded. (D&C 9:8.)

Another phrase by Nephi intensified my problem: "In the days that the prophecies of Isaiah shall be fulfilled men shall *know of a surety*, at the times when they shall come to pass." (2 Ne. 25:7; italics added.) Knowing that we are living in the days when the prophecies of Isaiah are being fulfilled indicated to me that something was wrong. Was the phrase "men shall know of a surety" a false prophecy? I would think, "I certainly do not know for a surety!" Nephi claimed, "They shall be of great worth unto them in the last days; for in that day shall they understand them." (2 Ne. 25:8.) Was he talking about a day later on in these "last days"? After all, who among us in these days understands and knows "of a surety"? How can the words of Isaiah be for our good when we do not understand them, in spite of the fact that Nephi declared, "For their [our] good have I written them"?

However, we are now living in a day of fulfillment. Great things are happening. All these words are being fulfilled! The number of firesides, sacrament meetings, and Education Week lectures on the book of Isaiah is continually increasing. Today, some are beginning to understand and love the words of Isaiah as never before.

A Commandment in Fulfillment

This increased interest, studying, understanding, and loving the words of Isaiah is a direct fulfillment of the great instructions given to the Nephites by the Savior after his resurrection. After quoting from several chapters of Isaiah, the Savior added this admonition: "And now, behold, I say unto you, that ye ought to search these things. Yea, a commandment I give unto you that ye search these things diligently; for great are the words of Isaiah." (3 Ne. 23:1.)

The Savior gave the reason Isaiah's words were great: "For surely he spake as touching all things concerning my people which are of the house of Israel; therefore it must needs be that he must speak also to the Gentiles." (3 Ne. 23:2.) These words of the Savior give us one of the grand keys in understanding Isaiah. The Savior proclaimed that Isaiah spoke of "all things concerning" his people (of the house of Israel), and then reasoned that therefore Isaiah was speaking concerning the Gentiles. We may therefore use this same reasoning to apply Isaiah's words to ourselves.

Elder McConkie stated, "Personally, I feel about Isaiah and his utterances the same way Nephi felt and think that if I expect to go where Nephi and Isaiah have gone, I had better speak their language, think their thoughts, know what they knew, believe and teach what they believed and taught, and live as they lived." (*Ensign*, Oct. 1973, p. 78.)

If the Savior and Nephi both stressed that the words of Isaiah were "of great worth" and "for our good," if the Savior commanded us to diligently search the words of Isaiah, and if they are evidently pertinent to our salvation, why are the words of Isaiah so profoundly hidden from our understanding? There are special reasons. These reasons have to do with who Isaiah was, who he was speaking to, and the nature of prophecy.

2
Who Was Isaiah?

Who was the prophet Isaiah? What status did he have among the prophets living in his day? Why is it that he has been so extensively quoted by other prophets throughout the New and Old Testaments and the Book of Mormon, and by the Savior? What kind of a prophet was he? When did he live and how extensive was his influence?

There are several special reasons why the prophet Isaiah was a prophet of such great renown. One biblical scholar by the name of Nagelsback stated, "Isaiah is the great Central-Prophet, ... the one on whom all later prophets lean as their greatest exemplar and highest prophetic authority." (Carl Nagelsback, *The Prophet Isaiah*, p. 2.) Nagelsback also stated that many scholars consider Isaiah as a prophet of the highest rank, authority, and esteem. Nagelsback explained, in reference to Isaiah, "he [who] stands highest, sees the furthest." He also explained that Isaiah was a master of the Hebrew language, using it with a power and ease unparalleled by any other prophet. He claimed that Isaiah brought the Hebrew language to the summit of its development, and that all rhetorical forms of art were at Isaiah's command.

From Whence Came Isaiah?
Almost nothing is known of Isaiah's birth and youth. The introduction to the book of Isaiah merely tells us that he was the son of Amoz. Who his father was, is likewise unknown. Some biblical scholars and Hebrew sages have suggested that he was related to King Amaziah, but no evidence can be found to support the claim. Some claim that Isaiah's father, Amoz, was a prophet, but give no

4

substantial evidence. Amoz may have been a prophet, but we have little evidence of it. There is one allusion to it in the extracanonical book, the Ascension of Isaiah (R. H. Charles, ed. and trans. [London: Adam and Charles Black, 1900]; see Appendix B). However, the allusions in Ascension 1:2 and 4:22 are not clear.

Some Latter-day Saint scholars have referred to Isaiah as a court prophet and have suggested that he was of royal birth, but this is also unsubstantiated. The fact that Isaiah had ready access to the kings of his day may have depended more on his prophetic call and character than on his relationship to the kings. It appears that Isaiah's access to the kings also depended on the particular king's righteousness. For example, there is much information and dialogue available between Isaiah and Hezekiah, opposed to available dialogue between Isaiah and the wicked kings Ahaz and Manasseh. In fact, according to Ascension 2:7-11, Isaiah spent much of his time during two years of Manasseh's reign in retreat, hiding in the mountains of Bethlehem.

Isaiah is referred to as a court prophet, or prophet statesman, but this is because of his ready access to the king. One of the most famous calls Isaiah made on King Ahaz was not in the king's court at all, but rather more on common ground. The famous call on Ahaz, when Isaiah delivered an unwanted message and prophecy of Christ's birth, was in the highway of the fuller's field at the end of the conduit of the upper pool. (Isa. 7:3.)

Biblical scholars, including some Latter-day Saints, have claimed that Isaiah's prophetic life was limited to the days when Uzziah, Jotham, Ahaz, and Hezekiah were kings of Judah. However, this may not be true. The reason scholars limit Isaiah's days is because of the introduction in Isaiah 1:1. This verse has been quoted as evidence that Isaiah died during the reign of King Hezekiah, since no other kings were mentioned. However, there is evidence that Isaiah lived longer and wrote more than what we have as the book of Isaiah. In 2 Chronicles 26:22 we read, "Now the rest of the acts of Uzziah, first and last, did Isaiah the prophet, the son of Amoz, write." Yet, the "rest of the acts of Uzziah, first and last," are not in the book of Isaiah. Therefore, many more scriptures and writings by Isaiah once existed. If the Ascension of Isaiah originally came from the prophet Isaiah, then King Manasseh, son of Hezekiah, must be added to the list of kings ruling during Isaiah's day. Confirmation that this may be the case is found in two sources in the early writings of the Jewish rabbis near the time of Christ, referred to as the Talmud. The Sanhedrin Talmud (Isadore Epstein, ed. and trans., *The Babylonian Talmud*, vol. 10, p. 702) states that Manasseh slew Isaiah. In the Yebamoth Talmud (p. 324), one early rabbi states that Isaiah was captured by Manasseh and sawn asunder. According to these evidences, Isaiah lived a few years longer than most scholars think.

Isaiah was a prophet of prophets, a prophet of the future and the restoration, a prophet of the latter days; he was a man with literary and poetic greatness, a prophet statesman, a great orator, and a man of exceeding courage.

Prophet of Prophets

There is plenty of evidence that the statement made by Nagelsback of the greatness of Isaiah's prophetic status is accurate. Elder Bruce R. McConkie stated, "Isaiah is a prophet's prophet; his words live in the hearts of those who themselves are authoring holy writ." (*Ensign*, Oct. 1973, p. 81.)

The fact that Isaiah was quoted by the Savior, both in the New Testament and in the Book of Mormon, is in itself ample evidence that Isaiah was a prophet of prophets. In addition, Isaiah is quoted in the New and Old Testaments and in the Book of Mormon more extensively than any other prophet. The prophet Nephi also spoke highly of Isaiah's words: "And now I, Nephi, write more of the words of Isaiah, for my soul delighteth in his words. For I will liken his words unto my people, and I will send them forth unto all my children, for he verily saw my Redeemer, even as I have seen him." (2 Ne. 11:2.)

There is also evidence that Isaiah was a prophet of prophets in his own day. In the Ascension of Isaiah, we are told that there were forty prophets and sons of the prophets who came from the villages, mountains, and plains to Jerusalem when they heard that Isaiah was coming from Galgala to call on King Hezekiah. According to this account, these came "to salute him and to hear his words. And that he might place his hands upon them, and that they might prophesy and that he might hear their prophecy: and they were all before Isaiah." (Asc. 6:4-5.) Among the prophets and sons of prophets were Micaiah, the aged Ananias, Joel, and

Josab. (Asc. 6:7.) This Josab appears to be Isaiah's son Shearjashub (Isa. 7:3), Jasub or Josab for short. Another indication that Isaiah was the prophet of these prophets is the fact that Isaiah gave instructions to the other prophets. For example, just prior to his death he instructed Joel, Micaiah, and other Old Testament prophets of his day, saying, "Go ye to the region of Tyre and Sidon; for for me only hath God mingled the cup." (Asc. 5:13.) (See Appendix B for a modern translation of the Ascension.)

Another aspect in which Isaiah was prophet of prophets is that of his call. Isaiah was called (Isa. 6) to a special mission, which he received by a special vision of the Lord in the temple. This may or may not have been his initial call as a prophet, although it is generally considered to be. The fact that the Lord appeared to Isaiah to personally give him his call seems greatly significant.

Another indication of Isaiah's greatness as a prophet is the vision Isaiah related to Hezekiah, Micaiah, and the rest of the prophets concerning his ascension to the seventh heaven, where he beheld the Son, the Father, the Holy Spirit, and all the righteous from the time of Adam (Abel, Seth, Enoch, etc.). In this vision Isaiah was told that he would receive his exaltation. He also beheld the birth and life of the Savior. (Asc. 3-11.) This vision of the life and death of the Savior may have been one of the sources of inspiration for the magnificent portrayal of the atonement in Isaiah 53:

> He is despised and rejected of men; a man of sorrows, and acquainted with grief: and we hid as it were our faces from him; he was despised, and we esteemed him not. (Isa. 53:3.)

> But he was wounded for our transgressions, he was bruised for our iniquities: the chastisement of our peace was upon him; and with his stripes we are healed.
> All we like sheep have gone astray; we have turned every one to his own way; and the Lord hath laid on him the iniquity of us all. (Isa. 53:5-6.)

> He shall see of the travail of his soul, and shall be satisfied: by his knowledge shall my righteous servant justify many; for he shall bear their iniquities. (Isa. 53:11.)

In fact, some of the evidence used by Manasseh's court in seeking to kill Isaiah was the accusation that Isaiah claimed to be greater than Moses, seeing greater things than Moses saw, having seen God. Manasseh's wicked supporters then used the same reasoning used by the majority of the religious sects today. They quoted Moses as having said that "no man can see God." For Isaiah to claim to have seen God was, to them, blasphemy, a sin worthy of death. (Asc. 3; Lev. 24:16.) This custom of the Jews was maintained in Judah down to and including the time of Christ and the first Christian martyr, Stephen. (Acts 7:22-37.)

The fact that Isaiah had beheld the Savior, evidently on more than one occasion, in addition to his conversing with angels, added emphasis to his high status as *the* prophet of his day. Nephi used this same fact as one of the reasons for Isaiah's greatness: "For he verily saw my Redeemer, even as I have seen him." (2 Ne. 11:2.) Since Isaiah had beheld such glorious things, and, in addition, received the promise of eternal life, he would naturally be an authority on such things. He would be an authority for all future generations on how to become sanctified, obtain eternal life, and prepare for the coming of Christ. It is understandable why Isaiah was referred to in the Ascension writings as the holy Isaiah. (Asc. 6:14.) A prophet who seals his life and testament with his blood, as Isaiah did, is held in high esteem by all future righteous saints and prophets. Thus, Isaiah was outstanding among the prophets, a prophet of prophets.

The Prophet of the Restoration

Elder Bruce R. McConkie referred to Isaiah as "the prophet of the restoration." (*Ensign*, Oct. 1973, p. 80.) This is readily understood when one considers the fact that over fifty-five of the sixty-six chapters in the book of Isaiah predict the restored gospel in the last days, including the coming forth of the Book of Mormon (chapter 29); Joseph Smith as the prophet of the latter-day gathering and the Restoration, and as an ensign to the people (chapters 11, 29, and 49); missionaries going to all the world (chapters 18 and 60); establishment of the Church (2:2-3; 54:2); and other events of the last days and millennial era.

What is the difference between Isaiah and Joseph Smith being the prophet of the Restoration? The word prophet implies foretelling or prophesying. Isaiah was the prophet *foretelling* the Restoration. Joseph Smith was the prophet *fulfilling* the prophecies of the Restoration. Thus, Joseph was fulfilling Isaiah's prophecies.

Isaiah was *the* Old Testament prophet of the last days. He

referred to the last days, and events relating to us, more than any other prophet in the Bible. Since Isaiah knew that the people of his day would not repent, his message of hope and redemption was primarily to the remnant of Israel who would come forth in the last days to accept the gospel. Since he "spake as touching all things concerning...the house of Israel" (3 Ne. 23:2), his prophecies describe our day. His special warning and admonition are for our best good. The Savior said that Isaiah spoke of *all* things concerning the house of Israel in the last days. (See 3 Ne. 23:1-2.) Isaiah not only described our day and the events of it, but told us of the future and what we must do to prepare for it. In fact, his prophecies are of such pertinent application to us in these days, that a more complete analysis of them will be found in the last two chapters and Appendix A of this book.

Poetic Greatness

The writings of Isaiah are great poetry. Sidney B. Sperry stated that Isaiah has no rival in the Old Testament in his versatility of expression and brilliance of imagery. (Sidney B. Sperry, *The Voice of Israel's Prophet,* p. 15.) Many of the Old Testament scholars indicate that the style of Isaiah is at the apex of Hebrew literary art. The great characteristics of Isaiah's literary writings observed by biblical scholars include his descriptive metaphors, beautifully picturesque illustrations, and richness of vocabulary. The great conservative scholar, Merrill Unger, claimed that "Isaiah...is the greatest of the Hebrew prophets and orators. For splendor of diction, brilliance of imagery, versatility and beauty of style, he is unequaled." (Merrill F. Unger, *Introductory Guide to the Old Testament,* p. 311.) Hebrew is one of the greatest, if not the greatest, of poetic languages. This poetic quality can be experienced as one reads the book of Isaiah in the Hebrew. The King James translation has marvelously retained much of the poetic nature. Although it is not as great as the Hebrew, it far exceeds other translations.

For example, the following passage moves the reader into a beautiful ecstasy of poetic grandeur. But since it was given in the Spirit, it can only be fully appreciated in the Spirit. It must be read with feeling, in anticipation of experiencing the sublime.

Hast thou not known?
Hast thou not heard,
That the everlasting God, the Lord,
The Creator of the ends of the earth,
Fainteth not, neither is weary?
There is no searching of his understanding.
He giveth power to the faint;
And to them that have no might he increaseth strength.
Even the youths shall faint and be weary,
And the young men shall utterly fall:
But they that wait upon the Lord shall renew their strength;
They shall mount up with wings as eagles;
They shall run, and not be weary;
And they shall walk, and not faint.
(Isa. 40:28-31.)

The frequent use of poetic metaphor throughout the book of Isaiah is found in these verses. Isaiah helps the reader "mount up with wings as eagles."

The book of Isaiah is a rich source of marvelous poetry. Isaiah's writing has a natural beauty void of formal rigor or painstaking form. One does not need to be schooled in the professional discipline of literature or art appreciation to enjoy Isaiah's literary qualities. The most uneducated person can receive the bounteous rewards of Isaiah's grandeur through reading by the Spirit. One impressive example is Isaiah 32:15-18. The phrases of these verses are marvelously beautiful. Reading aloud with feeling, one can almost vicariously experience Isaiah's magnificent spirit through the majestic language:

Until the spirit be poured upon us from on high,
And the wilderness be a fruitful field,
And the fruitful field be counted for a forest.
Then judgment shall dwell in the wilderness,
And righteousness remain in the fruitful field.
And the work of righteousness shall be peace;
And the effect of righteousness quietness and assurance for ever.
And my people shall dwell in a peaceable habitation,
And in sure dwellings, and in quiet resting places. (Isa. 32:15-18.)

The message is both profound and beautiful. One can feel power in this message. It makes the reader want to experience the fulfillment of this prophecy personally.

Even the condemning chastisements and rebukes are beautifully poetic:

Woe unto them that draw iniquity with cords of vanity,
And sin as it were with a cart rope:
Woe unto them that call evil good, and good evil;
That put darkness for light, and light for darkness;
That put bitter for sweet, and sweet for bitter!
Therefore as the fire devoureth the stubble,
And the flame consumeth the chaff,
So their root shall be as rottenness,
And their blossom shall go up as dust:
Because they have cast away the law of the Lord of hosts,
And despised the word of the Holy One of Israel. (Isa. 5:18, 20, 24.)

One needs but to read the book of Isaiah aloud in private from the Hebrew or from the King James Version to experience the poetic grandeur of Isaiah's style. It has been said that prophets are poets. When the Spirit gives one utterance, it is naturally beautiful; such is the "language of [the] fathers." (Mosiah 1:2.) Isaiah, a prophet of prophets, was also a poet of poets and an orator of orators.

Prophet of Great Courage

Isaiah showed great courage in his fearless warnings to the kings of Israel and the Gentile nations. His courage was forcefully evident in the warnings and judgments pronounced with "unwearyingness" upon those who resented his words. This "unwearyingness" is characteristic of the great and holy prophets. Nephi, son of Helaman, was given great power because he sought the Lord's will with such unwearyingness and feared not man. (Hel. 10:4-5.) What was said of Nephi is also true of Isaiah: "Thou hast not feared [man], and hast not sought thine own life, but hast sought my will, and to keep my commandments." (Hel. 10:4.)

One of the greatest evidences of Isaiah's superior courage is found in the record of his martyrdom. According to the Ascension, the prophet Isaiah told Hezekiah that his son Manasseh would put him (Isaiah) to death: "Isaiah said to Hezekiah the king . . . As the Lord liveth . . . and the Spirit which speaketh in me liveth, all these commands and these words will be made none effect by Manasseh thy son, and through the agency of his hands I shall depart mid the torture of my body.'' (Asc. 1:7.) This prophecy made King Hezekiah weep and want to put Manasseh to death to prevent him from killing the prophet of the Lord. But instead, Manasseh succeeded his father to the throne, and the time came when he fulfilled Isaiah's prophecies:

> And when Isaiah was being sawn in sunder, Belchira stood up accusing him, and all the false prophets stood up, laughing and rejoicing because of Isaiah. . . . And Belchira said to Isaiah: Say, I have lied in all that I have spoken, and also the ways of Manasseh are good and right; and the ways also of Belchira and of his associates are good . . . I will compel Manasseh to reverence thee. And Isaiah answered and said: So far as I have utterance, Condemned and accursed be thou and all thy powers and all thy house. For thou canst not take ought but the skin (flesh) of my body. So they seized and sawed in sunder, Isaiah, the son of Amoz, with a wooden saw. (Asc. 5:2-11.)

The greatness of Isaiah was not appreciated by Manasseh, his false prophets, and the people of his day. This was because Isaiah pronounced warnings and condemnations upon them. Even as late as A.D. 300, the Jewish leaders still did not fully appreciate Isaiah's greatness. They did not like his chastisements. Jewish leaders a few centuries after the time of Christ stated in the Mishnah, the writings of Jewish leaders, that Isaiah was put to death in the manner he was because of the way Isaiah talked to them as a people. They were offended when he said, "I dwell in the midst of a people of unclean lips." And yet these leaders overlooked the rest of the sentence and its greatness: "for mine eyes have seen the King, the Lord of hosts." (Isa. 6:5.)

The life and death of the prophet Isaiah has many similarities to that of the Savior, although Isaiah lived to be much older than the Savior. Isaiah's difficult life, rejection by his own people, sufferings and afflictions, greatness, and being put to death for his testimony all have common elements with the life of Christ. As one reads the following verses, he can see that they may be applied both to Isaiah and the Savior:

> And he hath made my mouth like a sharp sword;
> In the shadow of his hand hath he hid me,
> And made me a polished shaft;
> In the quiver hath he hid me; . . .

> Then I said, I have laboured in vain,
> I have spent my strength for nought, and in vain:
> Surely my judgment is with the Lord,
> And my reward with my God. (Isa. 49:2, 4.)

Although these and a few subsequent verses may be prophecy applicable more to Joseph Smith, they can nevertheless be applied to Isaiah, and thus have multiple fulfillment.

Now that we have considered who Isaiah was, we need to understand to whom he was speaking and the nature of prophecy.

3
Where the Critics Hid Isaiah

Attempts made by modern biblical scholars to explain Isaiah's words have instead had the effect of obscuring them. The majority of biblical scholars in the nineteenth and twentieth centuries are referred to as biblical critics. They seek to identify and explain biblical problems. Sometimes, as is the case with the book of Isaiah, they tend to create more problems than they solve.

Why have the majority of biblical scholars ended up making Isaiah even more confusing? Where have they hidden the real Isaiah whom we seek to know and understand? The answers to these questions can be found through understanding the manner of prophesying among the Jews.

Manner of Prophesying
The words of Isaiah have not only been hard for *us* to understand, but were also difficult for the Jews who lived comparatively close to the time of Isaiah. The prophet Nephi, approximately one hundred fifty to two hundred years after Isaiah, indicated that "Isaiah spake many things which were hard for many of my people to understand." (2 Ne. 25:1.) Nephi gave the reason for their lack of understanding as not knowing the manner of prophesying among the Jews.

The key to understanding the manner of prophesying among the Jews was given by Nephi: "For their works were works of darkness, and their doings were doings of abominations." (2 Ne. 25:2.) Therefore, the manner of prophesying among the Jews consisted of "the judgments of God" that were to "come upon all nations." (2 Ne. 25:3.)

Lehi's prophesying was also hard for some to understand.

Nephi said that his father "truly spake many great things unto them, which were hard to be understood, save a man should inquire of the Lord." (1 Ne. 15:3.) Because Laman and Lemuel's works were those of darkness and abomination, they could not understand the words of the prophets, even those of their own father, because they were "hard in their hearts, therefore they did not look unto the Lord as they ought." (1 Ne. 15:3.) Although Nephi said that the Jews could understand the words of Isaiah better than other people, anyone may reach a more complete understanding by inquiring of the Lord. (See 1 Ne. 15:3.)

This inquiring of the Lord includes changing oneself so as to overcome being hard of heart. Nephi said that the way to soften the heart is to "cry unto the Lord." The natural man, being an enemy to God, must yield to the enticings of the Spirit and deliberately seek a soft heart. (See Mosiah 3:19.) Nephi said, "I did cry unto the Lord; and behold he did visit me, and did soften my heart that I did believe all the words which had been spoken by my father; wherefore, I did not rebel against him like unto my brothers." (1 Ne. 2:16.) As one seeks the Lord to soften his heart, he believes the words of the prophets, instead of following man's natural tendency to rebel against them.

Two Reasons for Hiding

Men who do not seek a soft heart naturally reject revelation and rebel against the words of the prophets. For this reason, they seek to hide the words of Isaiah so as to avoid applying them to themselves.

There is a second reason the words of Isaiah are hidden. Biblical scholars and others have deliberately hidden the words of Isaiah in their transcribing and translating, and in their attempts to explain them. In fact, the prophet Isaiah, knowing the hearts of such men in the last days, predicted what these men would do to his prophecies. Isaiah, according to the Ascension of Isaiah, prophesied that "they will make of none effect the prophecy of the prophets which were before me, and these my visions also will they make of none effect, in order to speak after the impulse of their own heart." (Asc. 3:31.) There is ample evidence that the impulse of the scholars' hearts has been to reject the revelations, particularly Isaiah's.

Thus, the words of Isaiah are difficult for many to understand for two reasons. First, they do not seek to soften their hearts, and second, scholars and others have sought to hide the true meaning. Both reasons are caused by the natural man. The natural man seeks darkness instead of light, that his sins might be covered and hidden in darkness. When the sins of the natural man are brought to light, he becomes angry at, and even seeks to kill, the prophet who reveals them, be it Isaiah or the Savior himself.

Those Who Understand

There are those who understand Isaiah. Why is it that some do understand? Nephi indicated that there are two groups of people who understand the words of Isaiah: first, "the Jews do understand the things of the prophets," including those who have been "taught after the manner of the things of the Jews" (2 Ne. 25:5); and second, those who live in the latter days, since they live when "the prophecies of Isaiah shall be fulfilled." (2 Ne. 25:7.)

What do these two groups of people have in common? Nephi did not teach his people "the manner of the Jews" because their "works were works of darkness." Those who knew the manner of the Jews understood the words of Isaiah, at least to some extent. The common element in these two groups is that each lived in a day when the works of men of the world were works of darkness. The last days are also known as days when men's works will be "works of darkness," so much so that the Lord's coming is referred to as a day of vengeance: "For it is the day of the Lord's vengeance, and the year of recompences for the controversy of Zion." (Isa. 34:8.) Thus, those who understand the words of Isaiah live among, or know "concerning the manner of" those whose works are of darkness. It is as if to say, "Somehow those who understand must know of great wickedness to fully comprehend Isaiah's manner of prophesying."

Do Not Be Deceived

One day Alvin Rencher and Wayne Larsen received a letter that greatly surprised them. This particular letter was one of the many that came in response to the national news release about their Book of Mormon style analysis. They had reported evidence that the Book of Mormon was compiled from writings of several different authors or prophets. They also reported evidence that the Isaiah material in the Book of Mormon appeared to be from one and the same author. This strange letter they received cautioned them about saying anything about the Isaiah material in the Book of Mormon, the reason being that researchers of the world had reported that the last fifteen chapters of Isaiah had been written by a different author than the first chapters of Isaiah.

Some members of the Church have been disturbed by the critics who claim that the book of Isaiah was not all written by Isaiah. Some ask if Isaiah only wrote part of the book bearing his name. They wonder, if he did not, would all that we say about Isaiah and the book of Isaiah still be true? If Isaiah did not write all of the book of Isaiah, it would seem that the Book of Mormon is not true, since the Book of Mormon claims that Isaiah wrote the parts of his book that the critics claim Isaiah did not write. The answer to this problem is needed; it affects all else that follows concerning the prophecies in the book of Isaiah.

When confronted with this problem, Elder James E. Talmage of the Quorum of the Twelve laid it to rest in a simple and sufficient manner. (See *Conference Report*, Apr. 1929, pp. 45-49.) Elder Talmage informed his inquirers that he had searched out the authorship problem of the book of Isaiah enough to know assuredly that the book was written by the prophet Isaiah as claimed. The fact that both the Savior and Nephi attested to Isaiah being the author outweighed all other evidence.

Although one may know the answer to the problem, he may be curious as to what the results would be if he were to tackle the claims and evidences of critics from a scientific basis. This chapter is for those interested in such results.

Theories of the Critics

The majority of biblical scholars claim that most of the book of Isaiah was written by someone other than Isaiah. It all began back in A.D. 1100 when a Jewish commentator by the name of Moses ben Samuel, Ibn-Gekatilla, denied that Isaiah was the author of certain chapters. (Edward J. Young, *An Introduction to the Old Testament*, p. 199.) Later, Ibn Ezra, in A.D. 1167, also questioned the authorship of certain sections in the book of Isaiah. (George A. Buttrick et al. (eds.), *The Interpreter's Bible 5*, p. 382.)

This theory grew until some scholars claimed that the book of Isaiah was a compilation of works from many authors and many periods of time. (John L. McKenzie, *Dictionary of the Bible.*) However, the early Jewish tradition maintained that Isaiah was the author of the entire book. (Sidney B. Sperry, *The Voice of Israel's Prophet*, pp. 75-76.)

A scholar by the name of Horn stated that other external evidence for the unity of the book of Isaiah came chiefly from two sources—the apocryphal work, Ecclesiasticus, and the Dead Sea Scrolls of Isaiah. (Siegfried H. Horn, *Seventh-Day Adventist Bible Dictionary*, pp. 509-10.) However, Horn agreed that the greatest evidence of unity consisted of the statements made by Jesus and the New Testament writers.

One of the leading conservative scholars, Robinson, stated that one fundamental belief of the critics underlies all the criticisms of Old Testament prophecy. (McKenzie, *Dictionary of the Bible*, p. 379.) This belief is that a prophet always limits his prophecies to the present needs of the people and not beyond the horizon of his own day. The classical problem cited by critics of the Old Testament is the prophecy in Isaiah chapters 44 and 45 concerning King Cyrus of Persia. They argue that a prophet could not prophesy in such detail as giving the name of King Cyrus nearly two centuries before he was born.

Sidestepping by the Critics

The conservative scholars insist that the prophet Isaiah actually predicted events related to King Cyrus and the captivity of Israel by Babylonia. They cite other Old Testament prophecies that span future generations to foretell specific names and events, such as those found in 1 Kings 13, Ezekiel 26, Micah 5:2, and Zechariah 9. These scholars also cite the prophecy that foretold the name of King Josiah and his religious reform more than three centuries prior to his birth (1 Kgs. 13:1-2); the mention of Bethlehem by Micah (Micah 5:2), a contemporary of Isaiah, as the birthplace of the Messiah; and the yoke of Tyre under the Babylonians as promised by Ezekiel (26) and Zechariah (9).

The great conservative scholar Harrison explained that the prophecy by an unnamed prophet foretelling the events of King Josiah (1 Kgs. 13:1-2) was particularly embarrassing to the critical scholars. Harrison pointed out that because the critics insisted that prophecy could not predict the future, they tried to divert the critical gaze from that of prophecy in the book of Isaiah to that of literary style. (R. K. Harrison, *Introduction to the Old Testament*, p. 765.)

Why is it that the majority of Old Testament scholars cannot accept the fact that prophets do foresee future events? Prophecy is real to a Latter-day Saint. But since the scholars cannot accept revelation, they cannot accept prophecy. And why is it they cannot accept revelation? To accept revelation is to accept the Revelator, namely Jesus Christ. John the Revelator stated that a testimony of Jesus is the spirit of prophecy. (Rev. 19:3.) Naturally the Jews could not accept Jesus as the Christ and revelator, but what is the problem with the Christian scholars?

According to the Lord, everyone is born with the light of Christ. (See John 1:9.) Any man following that Light would be led to Christ and the true Church:

> And the Spirit giveth light to every man that cometh into the world; and the Spirit enlighteneth every man through the world, that hearkeneth to the voice of the Spirit. And every one that hearkeneth to the voice of the Spirit cometh unto God, even the Father. And the Father teacheth him of the covenant.... (D&C 84:46-48.)

> All those who...are willing to take upon them the name of Jesus Christ...and truly manifest by their works that they have received of the Spirit of Christ unto the remission of their sins, shall be received by baptism into his church. (D&C 20:37.)

Thus, the reason scholars cannot accept revelation is that they reject the light of Christ. Elder Bruce R. McConkie stated, "The recognizable operation of this Spirit (light of Christ) in enlightening the mind and striving to lead men to do right is called *conscience*." (*Mormon Doctrine*, p. 156.) The natural man is an enemy to God and does not want to repent and follow the Lord. Therefore, most men reject revelation and follow the impulse of their own heart, instead of following the enticings of the Holy Spirit. (See Mosiah 3:19.) In so doing, the so-called scholars make the prophecies of Isaiah of "none effect," fulfilling the ancient prophecy:

> For there will be great jealousy in the last days; for everyone will say what is pleasing in his own eyes. And they will make of none effect the prophecy of the prophets which were before me, and these my visions also will they make of none effect, in order to speak after the impulse of their own heart. (Asc. 3:30-31.)

The literal and precise fulfillment today of this very descriptive prophecy of the last days is ample evidence that the author was a true prophet. This is the same reason that many scholars of our day believe that Christ was not divine, or have many other false concepts about God and Christ.

What About the Dead Sea Scrolls?

Since the discovery of the Dead Sea Scrolls in 1947, considerable emphasis has been given to them by some individuals. Emphasis has especially been placed on the fact that the entire book of Isaiah was among the scrolls. Some individuals have stressed that this is evidence of the authenticity of the book of Isaiah having come from the prophet by that name.

However, such claims are not warranted in consideration of the dating of the scrolls. The scrolls are dated approximately 150 B.C. This is not early enough to serve as evidence that the book of Isaiah was written by Isaiah.

These scrolls have been most accurately dated by use of coins found with the scrolls. The dates on the coins place the date of the scrolls in the first or second century B.C.

The so-called scholars claim that the non-Isaiah portions of the book were written by scribes and others between Isaiah's day and the fourth century B.C. (Larry L. Adams, *A Statistical Style Analysis of the Book of Isaiah in Relation to the Isaiah Problem*, pp. 12-39.) Thus, the Dead Sea Scrolls and the book of Isaiah could have come from the same source and still be after the fourth century B.C. In fact, Rosenbloom's analysis indicates that both manuscripts may have had a common origin. (Joseph R. Rosenbloom, *The Dead Sea Isaiah Scroll*.) The major problem is that this common origin has not been dated early enough to refute the biblical critics.

What Difference Does It Make?

There are three important reasons why we must know who

wrote the book of Isaiah, especially if we are to fully understand it:

1. To know if the author was a prophet and if the writings are scripture.
2. If the author is Isaiah, knowing so will help us understand the book. It will help us to interpret the various prophecies in relation to each other, in relation to Isaiah's major doctrinal themes, and in relation to his call and his goal of preparing a latter-day remnant for the Second Coming.
3. If the author is Isaiah, it would stand as evidence to the truthfulness of the Book of Mormon, since the Book of Mormon quotes various sections of the book of Isaiah, attributing them to Isaiah.

Authorship of the book of Isaiah also stands as evidence of the truthfulness of the New Testament and the Savior himself, since Jesus and other New Testament writers quoted from the disputed sections of Isaiah, attributing them to Isaiah.

If the disputed sections quoted from the book of Isaiah were not written by Isaiah, then the words from the Book of Mormon, the New Testament, and the Savior would not have been inspired. This would serve as evidence in favor of those who do not want to believe in the Book of Mormon or in Jesus as the Christ. Of course, the real solution to this problem is that of revelation. An absolute answer may be obtained by inquiring of the Lord, as Nephi (1 Ne. 10:19), Moroni (Moro. 10:4), James (James 1:5), and others have challenged us to do. But since the majority of scholars profess not to believe in revelation, this challenge is not acceptable to them. They therefore divert the authorship argument to that of literary style in the book of Isaiah.

A Scientific Approach

What is the scientific approach to a problem? Simply stated, it is to search out all available evidence, pro and con, to see where the weight of evidence rests. Often, some of the evidence must be put to an appropriate test to see if it is valid, and to determine its weight in relation to other evidence. In fact, some types of evidence outweigh all the rest put together.

Where would we start for a scientific approach to an analysis of the literary style of the book of Isaiah? What evidence exists? The Old Testament critics claim that the style of speaking and writing are different in the different sections of the book of Isaiah. Some critics have insisted that no literary evidence exists for authorship unity of the book. One German critic, Fohrer, claimed that all literary evidence points to multiple authorship. (Georg Fohrer, *Introduction to the Old Testament*, p. 385.) The German critics at the time of the Nazi regime were foremost in fighting to divide up the authorship of the book of Isaiah.

The critics (by far in the majority) emphasize the literary differences among various sections of the book of Isaiah, and the conservatives the similarities. Conservative scholars who defend the authorship unity of the book have presented extensive rebuttals to the arguments of the divisionists. Disagreement has not only been strong between the two biblical schools of thought, but also within the critics' camp itself. In fact, little or no agreement as to the extent of the partitioning of the book can be found among the critics. (Yehuda T. Radday, "Isaiah and the Computer: A Preliminary Report," *Computers and the Humanities 5*, pp. 65-66; Adams, *Statistical Style Analysis of the Book of Isaiah*, pp. 10-42.) As one modern critic, Radday, recognized, the problem of identity of authorship is not determined by observing whether two texts are similar or not, but to what extent. (Yehuda T. Radday, "Two Computerized Statistical-Linguistic Tests Concerning the Unity of Isaiah," *Journal of Biblical Literature*, p. 324.) One critic, Gottwald, claimed that "it is one of the assured results of modern biblical science that chapters 50-66 were not written by the Prophet Isaiah." (Norman K. Gottwald, *A Light to the Nations: An Introduction to the Old Testament*, p. 400.) This claim and many others were put to the test and found to be completely unsupported. (Adams, *Statistical Style Analysis of the Book of Isaiah*, pp. 19-23.)

After two years of research of all available literature on the book of Isaiah, I discovered that only one out of ten scholars was in the conservative camp. (Adams, *Statistical Style Analysis of the Book of Isaiah*, pp. 19-23.) Since the scholars in the critics' camp claimed that the reason for dividing up the book of Isaiah was its literary style, the evidence concerning authorship could be tested using the computer and statistical analyses. Rates of literary usage, such as unique wording and other habits of speech or writing, could be identified and tabulated by a computer to conduct an authorship style analysis on the book of Isaiah compared with other Old Testament authors. This I did for claims made by both conservatives and divisionists.

Moving a Mount Everest

The file containing the comprehensive log of all claims and arguments obtained on the Isaiah authorship problem was a large one, filling a two-foot filing drawer. Since there were so many claims by both critics and conservatives, analyzing these claims was almost like moving an enormous mountain bare-handed. In fact, it would have been impossible were it not for certain computer techniques.

A team of thirty-five researchers at Brigham Young University, working three years, began by coding the Hebrew text of the book of Isaiah and a stratified random sample of verses from eleven other Old Testament books. The coded text was transferred to computer cards and tapes. The researchers involved in the project included Hebrew scholars, linguists, computer programmers, statisticians, computer keypunch typists, research secretaries, and other research specialists. They were assisted by the BYU computer center, graduate school, and religion department.

In addition to the full text of the book of Isaiah in Hebrew, other literary works were put on computer tape: parts of eleven other Old Testament books in Hebrew, the full text of the Book of Mormon, the full text of the Doctrine and Covenants, and large portions from the writings of the famous English poet, Thomas Carlyle.

Over three hundred computer programs were written to perform the analytical phase of this study. The three hundred computer programs were placed on computer tapes. Several computer programs were submitted to the computer daily, as days grew into weeks, and weeks into months. After a number of months, computer center personnel began to notice that this project was monopolizing a great deal of computer time. In addition, nearly one hundred computer tapes were tied up in the project. These tapes were needed to meet the needs of other departments on campus.

Some of the computer programs used in the analysis were extremely complicated and involved. One program took eight to twelve hours to operate, transforming and comparing sets of literary characteristics as it progressed from verse to verse, chapter to chapter, and book to book. This program was used to analyze the rate of repetition of scriptural phrases. Some conservative scholars claimed that Isaiah had a tendency to quote himself. This program was used to check the extent to which this claim was true. Most computer programs run for only a few seconds. When this complex, time-consuming program began to run, the computer operators naturally thought something had gone wrong with the program, and "dumped" it after a few minutes. They thought that the program must have made the computer run in an endless loop.

The program was resubmitted to the computer, and the computer operators were assured that it had not "gone into a loop." They were informed that it was a very lengthy program, and to "please let it run until it terminated." However, it was again dumped after forty-five minutes of operation. We finally had to submit the program to the computer at night, using a special operator, to get it to run the full eight to twelve hours.

A director of the computer center had asked from time to time if we could release at least half of the 100 computer tapes that we had tied up in our research. However, each time we were forced to inform him that we were unable to release the tapes yet. Finally, one of the directors came up to my office wanting to know if we would release the tapes. We found ourselves against what seemed to be an overwhelming barrier. We again explained that we were in no position to meet the request. We stepped into the office library, where we had filed thousands of sheets of computer printout. He saw the whole wall, shelf after shelf, of computer printout filed by section according to the type of literary analysis. To stop now would be to waste all that work. Scanning the voluminous printouts representing many hundreds of hours of work, he shook his head as if to ask, "What project in the whole world is worth this much?"

After explaining the purpose of the project, I exclaimed, "If the results of this study turn out to be evidence that the book of Isaiah was written by a single author, the truthfulness of the Book of Mormon will once more be confirmed! All the critics would be put to the acid test!" We then indicated to him that this same type of evidence would also bear witness to the truthfulness of the New Testament and of the Savior. "But," I pleaded, "we need just a little more time." As this good brother contemplated the implications of this research, his face lit up, and he said, "Okay! But please *hurry!*" We did hurry, using a twenty-four-hour schedule with various shifts of computer programmers and other researchers. Finally, within a couple of weeks, the vast results began to flow in.

As I anxiously pored over the results, I could hardly believe my eyes! I was completely overwhelmed at such strong evidence of unity, of single authorship, of the book of Isaiah in the literary style analysis! I distinctly recall sinking into my chair, so weak I could not stand, and the tears dropping to the computer paper. It had all been worth it!

There were several possible outcomes. We could have been following wrong leads, ending up with no evidence, for or against. Our instruments (computerized statistical formulas, in this case) could have been inadequate to uncover the most pertinent evidence. For example, we had previously had a major problem with a statistical routine doing what it was constructed to do. It could not seem to handle the specified task.

In addition, we had realized during the preliminary analysis for the research design, that the book of Isaiah was undoubtedly an abridgment from many other records originally written by Isaiah or his scribe. It was possible that the original record was Isaiah's, but that scribes or later prophets could have made the abridgment. There is some evidence that a later transcriber altered the text, at least to the extent of omitting parts. The extent to which such changes from the original text could have camouflaged the original style of the prophet Isaiah was not known. So when the literary style analysis resulted in such strong evidence that the book of Isaiah originated from a single author, it was very surprising and overwhelming.

Literary style in Hebrew is much more amenable to computerized analysis than is English. There is a Hebrew characteristic referred to as a *function prefix.* The function prefix can be used to identify many of the speech patterns unique to a given author. For example, it was discovered that "and it came to pass" was an idiomatic phrase consisting of a unique function prefix. The function prefixes in the book of Isaiah were one of the strongest evidences of single authorship.

In general, the claims made by the critics are not supported by the results of the research; to the contrary, the results tend to support the conservative arguments. Some minor claims by the critics are true, but not their arguments against single authorship. For example, a change in context or topics from one chapter or section to another was not found to be substantial evidence for change in authors. Likewise, some claims by conservative scholars were not found to be true. For example, nearly half of the conjugation prefixes identified by one conservative scholar as being unique to Isaiah were not found to support his claim.

In addition, the results of this study did not exclude the possibility of minor changes in the text, or even incidental additions to the text. However, such changes were evidently not significant enough to alter the overall style of the original author.

Invalid Attempts by Other Researchers

In the meantime, two different Jewish researchers in Israel had attempted a statistical style analysis of the book of Isaiah. They independently concluded that the book was written by at least two different authors. The more comprehensive work of the two scholars was that by Radday, who had concluded that there was only one chance in ten thousand that the first part of the book of Isaiah was written by the same author who wrote the second part. (Yehuda T. Radday, "Two Computerized Statistical-Linguistic Tests Concerning the Unity of Isaiah," *Journal of Biblical Literature*, p. 324.) However, his research was based upon several false assumptions. For example, Radday made the assumption that since Isaiah was living in a time of war, all of his prophecies and writings would be couched in war terminology. He also assumed that a person's manner of writing is the same regardless of whom he is writing to, be it his wife, a king, another prophet, or a group of wicked people. Since both Radday's and Kasher's approaches were based on unacceptable assumptions, the first part of our research entailed a test of their approach. It consisted of an analysis depicting how false conclusions can come from false assumptions.

We applied the same assumptions Radday and Kasher used, on literature for which we knew the author, on a few sections of the Doctrine and Covenants that came from Joseph Smith, and on various writings of Thomas Carlyle. Using their approach, we came up with the same type of conclusions Radday and Kasher did: that Thomas Carlyle could not have written the works that Thomas Carlyle wrote. The so-called evidence was even stronger than for Isaiah—we found only one chance in ten billion that Carlyle wrote what he wrote. The same results were found for the sections of the Doctrine and Covenants that came from the Prophet Joseph.

These results indicated that the approach used by these two researchers could not help but come up with the wrong conclusions. This was the same kind of approach that A. Q. Morton used when he claimed that the book of Hebrews and a number of sections from the other epistles of Paul in the New Testament were not written by Paul. (A. Q. Morton and James McLeman, *Paul, the Man and the Myth.*)

After spending some time in the arena with the higher critics of the Old Testament, I was confident that the critics' position would not allow them to publish, let alone accept as fact, the results of my study. Upon completing the research and an article reporting the results, I took a copy of the article to Brother Hugh Nibley to ask him if he thought that the editors would publish it in the *Journal of Biblical Literature.* Brother Nibley looked at the article and then replied, "JBL? Chicago? No! They would never publish it!" I thanked him and turned to leave, saying that I did not think they would, either, and just wanted to confirm the fact that it was a waste of time to submit it. But he quickly replied, "Oh no! You must submit it! You must give them a chance to reject it." So we submitted it, and the editor rejected it, with this conclusion: "We cannot understand the article, and besides, it is contrary to our convictions." Now how did they know it was contrary to their convictions if they could not understand the article? Of course, they realized from the summary that the article supported the unity of the book of Isaiah, and I knew that they would not publish any evidence that was contrary to "the impulse of their own heart." (Asc. 3:31.)

Some time later, this same editor was at Brigham Young University as a summer term exchange professor. Since his office was only a few doors down the hall from mine, I dropped in one day and showed him the article to refresh his memory. Then I asked him about it. He reconfirmed that it could not be published in their field. He used the type of reasoning that I was confident he would use. He claimed that there was not one living scholar today that accepted the unity of the book of Isaiah, and so there was no use to publish anything to the contrary.

Although I could have named him several living scholars who *did* believe in the unity of the book of Isaiah (Merrill Unger, for example), I knew that it was no use to argue with a man with a closed mind. He preferred to follow the stampede of the majority of biblical scholars, regardless of which direction it took them, rather than to stand in the lone plains of rejection—rejection as a scholar by the rest of the so-called scholars. The article has, however, been published in a more scientific journal. (L. La Mar Adams and Alvin C. Rencher, "The Popular Critical View of the Isaiah Problem in Light of Statistical Style Analysis," *Computer Studies in the Humanities and Verbal Behavior,* pp. 149-57); in *BYU Studies* (L. La Mar Adams and Alvin C. Rencher, "A Computer Analysis of Isaiah Authorship Problem," *BYU Studies,* pp. 94-102); and in the *Ensign* (Dec. 1973, pp. 58-59).

After the research was reported in the *Ensign,* I visited Jay Todd, the editor of the *Ensign,* and told him that what needed to be published next was an article on understanding the book of Isaiah. He suggested that I write up a proposal, which I did; then I delivered it to him. A week later I dropped back to ask him what he thought of the proposal. He was impressed with it. In addition, he indicated that they planned to ask Elder Bruce R. McConkie to write the article, which he did; it was subsequently published in the *Ensign.* (Bruce R. McConkie, "Ten Keys to Understanding Isaiah," *Ensign,* Oct. 1973, pp. 78-83.) I thought, "What an appropriate culmination!"

The results of this research and related experiences confirmed the unity of the book of Isaiah, added testimony to the truthfulness of the Book of Mormon and the New Testament, and confirmed the words of Isaiah that men in the last days would make the words of the prophets of none effect.

4
Keys to Understanding Isaiah

Can Isaiah really be understood? There are special keys that unlock the doors, allowing the light of Isaiah's words to break forth as the morning sun. The Prophet Joseph Smith from time to time gave what he called grand or great keys in understanding the scriptures. Joseph said, "I have a key by which I understand the scriptures." (HC 5:261.) Although the words of Isaiah have been hidden from our understanding, a few keys are available to solve this problem. These are simple keys, but without their proper application, comprehending the book of Isaiah is beyond our grasp.

There are two types of keys: those that may be immediately applied, and those that are developed over a period of time through practice and application. As we use these keys, the words of Isaiah will become even more meaningful to us.

Keys with Immediate Application
1. *Isaiah's prophecies are primarily about the last days.* Approximately eighty to ninety percent of Isaiah's prophecies are directly applicable to our day.
2. *Read with feeling.* Read with the intention of getting an overall feeling for what Isaiah is describing, without getting hung up on specific wording.
3. *Read Isaiah's prophecies aloud.* One feels the poetic beauty of Isaiah's prophecies better when reading orally.

These three keys are easy to use and understand, yet the results of application are greatly rewarding.

1. *Isaiah's prophecies are primarily about the last days.* Elder Sterling W. Sill declared, "Much of the writings of Isaiah concerns

our own day." (*Conference Report*, Apr. 1966, p. 19.) The
Prophet Joseph explained that a key he used to understand the
scriptures was to ask himself what the question or situation was
that evoked the prophecy, answer, or parable.

This key may be applied to the writings of Isaiah. For example,
Jesus commanded us to study the prophecies of Isaiah diligently.
(3 Ne. 23:1.) We might ask, "Why study Isaiah diligently?" The
obvious answer is, "For our good and benefit." Jesus added,
"...for surely he spake as touching all things concerning...the
house of Israel." (2 Ne. 23:2.) Therefore, he spoke of things concerning the Latter-day Saints. Nephi did the same thing when he
likened the words of Isaiah unto his people for their profit. (2 Ne.
11:2.)

Thus, a golden key to comprehending the words of Isaiah
would be to apply them to our day, to the Latter-day Saints, and
to our own lives. Elder Bruce R. McConkie emphasized that "we
cannot overstate or overstress the plain, blunt reality that he
[Isaiah] is in fact the prophet of the restoration...who foresaw
our day." (*Ensign*, Oct. 1973, p. 81.)

In at least 61 of the 66 chapters, Isaiah tells of God's dealings
with his children in the last days. The people of Isaiah's day were
so wicked that Isaiah's only hope for a righteous people was a
latter-day remnant of the house of Israel who would read and
accept his message. In fact, Isaiah was told to record his
prophecies for the last days: "Now go, write it before them in a
table, and note it in a book, that it may be for the latter day unto
eternity." (Isa. 30:8.)

Since Isaiah was called to preach to a stubborn-hearted people,
his prophecies were more for the benefit of the Latter-day Saints
than they were for the people of Isaiah's days. It is as though we
find Isaiah seeing through the events of his day, clear down
through the ages to the remnant in the last days. The following
figure is a depiction of Isaiah's prophecies to the house of Israel in
the eighth century B.C. and to the house of Israel in the nineteenth
and twentieth centuries A.D.

Thus, Isaiah's prophecies are either of the last days or can
usually be applied to both Isaiah's days and the last days. (See
Appendix A.)

There are three elements of most prophetic messages: (1) the

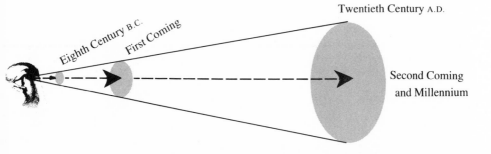

call, (2) the warning, and (3) the hope. The call is a call of repentance, a call to come unto the Savior. The warning is not only of curses for disobedience, but blessings for obedience as well. For example: "If ye be willing and obedient, ye shall eat the good of the land: but if ye refuse and rebel, ye shall be devoured with the sword: for the mouth of the Lord hath spoken it." (Isa. 1:19-20.)

Prophetic warnings of what will happen if we do not repent are, in a way, also a call to repentance:

> Therefore I command you to repent—repent, lest I smite you with the rod of my mouth and by my wrath, and by my anger, and your sufferings be sore—how sore you know not, how exquisite you know not, yea, how hard to bear you know not. For behold, I, God, have suffered these things for all, that they might not suffer if they would repent; But if they would not repent they must suffer even as I. (D&C 19:15-17.)

Isaiah's descriptive warning of punishment is a call to repentance: "For by fire and by his sword will the Lord plead with all flesh: and the slain of the Lord shall be many." (Isa. 66:16.)

The hope is for many things: (1) salvation through Christ, (2) the second coming of the Lord, and (3) the millennial era.

An example of the first hope proclaimed by Isaiah is the following prophecy concerning Christ's first advent and taking the gospel to those in the spirit prison:

> The Spirit of the Lord God is upon me; because the Lord hath anointed me to preach good tidings unto the meek; he hath sent me to bind up the brokenhearted, to proclaim liberty to the captives, and the opening of the prison to them that are bound. (Isa. 61:1.)

An example of the second and third hopes is:

> The sun shall be no more thy light by day; neither for brightness shall the
> moon give light unto thee: but the Lord shall be unto thee an everlasting
> light, and thy God thy glory. Thy sun shall no more go down; neither shall
> thy moon withdraw itself: for the Lord shall be thine everlasting light, and
> the days of thy mourning shall be ended. (Isa. 60:19-20.)

Isaiah's calling to prepare a people for the Second Coming was not fulfilled in his day. His mission was to prepare a "chosen seed" as a future remnant to meet the Lord at his second coming. His mission is hopefully fulfilled in us. Is it any wonder that the Savior gave us a commandment to diligently seek the words of Isaiah? It is easy to see that "great are the words of Isaiah." (3 Ne. 23:1.) If by his words we would know how to prepare to meet the Savior, Isaiah's prophecies would certainly be "of great worth unto [us] in the last days." (2 Ne. 25:8.) Through us in the last days, the prophecies of Isaiah shall be fulfilled. (2 Ne. 25:7.)

2. *Read with feeling.* When one reads with the intention of getting an overall feeling for what Isaiah is describing in a certain chapter or passage, one is not so apt to get lost or hung up on peculiar wording. This approach helps in several ways. First and foremost, as one reads by feeling, that person becomes more sensitive to the Spirit. This is a mechanical way of becoming sensitive to the promptings of the Spirit in reading, especially if one has asked for the Spirit. Second, reading by feeling helps one to skim over or ignore words and phrases that are mistranslations. Third, it helps one to at least obtain a general understanding of the message, even though unfamiliar words are used. And fourth, Isaiah tends to use a number of verses to paint a verbal picture of his message. When reading with feeling, one is more apt to be lead through Isaiah's complete message.

At an educational research convention, a researcher from an eastern university took advantage of the occasion to ask me about Isaiah. This good brother told me that he had heard of my work on the book of Isaiah, and asked if I could tell him in five minutes how to understand the book. We both laughed, and then I had a magnificent idea. "I am going to take you up on that challenge," I replied. Standing in front of my motel room door I told him that I would give him two keys to understanding Isaiah, and then I would have him come into my room and test his usage of those two keys on a certain chapter.

For five minutes we discussed the two keys. First, that eighty to ninety percent of Isaiah's prophecies are applicable to the last days; and second, the words of Isaiah must be read with feeling, to avoid getting hung up on the wording. We then stepped into the room, sat down at the table, and opened the Bible to Isaiah, chapter 18. I asked this brother to begin reading, concentrating on using these two keys. After he had read three verses, I stopped him to have him tell me what Isaiah had been talking about. He replied that he appeared to be talking about the missionaries in the last days going out to gather in scattered Israel. "Precisely!" I replied. "You see, it works!" I then asked him to reread the first two verses of chapter 18 again, and I pointed out to him that the translation in these verses tends to confuse the average reader unless he ignores the wording and reads using the two keys. These two verses could be termed mistranslations. A more correct translation of these verses compared to the King James Version is:

Corrected Translation	King James
Hail to the land shaped like wings, which is beyond the rivers of Ethiopia (beyond "our world" and ocean.) Which sends representatives by sea, in a gulp-measure over the face of the waters, saying, Go ye swift messengers, to a nation scattered and peeled ...(Isa. 18:1-2.)	Woe to the land shadowing with wings, which is beyond the rivers of Ethiopia: That sendeth ambassadors by the sea, even in vessels of bulrushes upon the waters, saying, Go, ye swift messengers, to a nation scattered and peeled, to a people terrible from their beginning hitherto; a nation meted out and trodden down, whose land the rivers have spoiled! (Isa. 18:1-2.)

When one reads by feeling, not getting hung up on specific words, he does not always need the more accurate translations. During the 1979 BYU Campus Education Week, President Marion G. Romney emphasized that we should not hide the teachings of the Old Testament by getting lost in the chaff that comes from the transcribers and translators.

3. *Read Isaiah's prophecies aloud.* Evidently, most of Isaiah's prophecies were given orally and make more sense when read aloud. But a more aesthetic reason is that one can feel the heavenly, poetic beauty of Isaiah's writings when reading aloud:

> How beautiful upon the mountains are the feet of him that bringeth good tidings, that publisheth peace; that bringeth good tidings of good, that publisheth salvation; that saith unto Zion, Thy God reigneth! Thy watchmen shall lift up the voice; with the voice together shall they sing: for they shall see eye to eye, when the Lord shall bring again Zion. Break forth into joy, sing together, ye waste places of Jerusalem: for the Lord hath comforted his people, he hath redeemed Jerusalem. (Isa. 52:7-9.)

Reading such a beautiful passage aloud almost makes one want to sing. In fact, a number of verses from the book of Isaiah have been put to song, and are part of the most beautiful music in the world, especially those in Handel's *Messiah*:

> The people that walked in darkness have seen a great light: they that dwell in the land of the shadow of death, upon them hath the light shined. Thou hast multiplied the nation, and...increased the joy: they joy before thee according to the joy in harvest, and as men rejoice when they divide the spoil. For thou hast broken the yoke of his burden, and the staff of his shoulder, the rod of his oppressor, as in the day of Midian. For every battle of the warrior is with confused noise, and garments rolled in blood; but this shall be with burning and fuel of fire. For unto us a child is born, unto us a son is given: and the government shall be upon his shoulder: and his name shall be called Wonderful, Counsellor, The mighty God, The everlasting Father, The Prince of Peace. Of the increase of his government and peace there shall be no end, upon the throne of David, and upon his kingdom, to order it, and to establish it with judgment and with justice from henceforth even for ever. The zeal of the Lord of hosts will perform this. The Lord sent a word into Jacob, and it hath lighted upon Israel. (Isa. 9:2-8.)

One can hardly read this masterpiece without being touched by its power and spirit.

Chapter 12 is of a little different nature, but is referred to as one of Isaiah's songs. It is a song of praise from which we learn some of the characteristics of a redeemed person "shouting praises" to the Lord. Nephi said that this type of praise is an earmark of a person who has experienced true repentance, being born of fire and the Spirit. (2 Ne. 31:13.) By reading the whole chapter aloud, one can feel the force and feeling of Isaiah's "shouting praises" unto the Lord:

> And in that day thou shalt say, O Lord, I will praise thee: though thou wast angry with me, thine anger is turned away, and thou comfortedst me.

> Behold, God is my salvation; I will trust, and not be afraid: for the Lord JEHOVAH is my strength and my song; he also is become my salvation. Therefore with joy shall ye draw water out of the wells of salvation. And in that day shall ye say, Praise the Lord, call upon his name, declare his doings among the people, make mention that his name is exalted. Sing unto the Lord; for he hath done excellent things: this is known in all the earth. Cry out and shout, thou inhabitant of Zion: for great is the Holy One of Israel in the midst of thee. (Isaiah, ch. 12.)

Whole chapters may profitably be read aloud, such as chapters 52 through 55; or merely a few verses may be read by themselves, but the power and beauty still remain:

> For as the rain cometh down, and the snow from heaven, and returneth not thither, but watereth the earth, and maketh it bring forth and bud, that it may give seed to the sower, and bread to the eater: So shall my word be that goeth forth out of my mouth: it shall not return unto me void, but it shall accomplish that which I please, and it shall prosper in the thing whereto I sent it. For ye shall go out with joy, and be led forth with peace: the mountains and the hills shall break forth before you into singing, and all the trees of the field shall clap their hands. Instead of the thorn shall come up the fir tree, and instead of the brier shall come up the myrtle tree: and it shall be to the Lord for a name, for an everlasting sign that shall not be cut off. (Isa. 55:10-13.)

Hebrew is a natural poetic language, perhaps because it is the language of the early prophets. It may also be that Hebrew is related to the Adamic language, the pure and undefiled language. (Moses 6:6.) Moroni stated, "If we could have written in Hebrew, behold, ye would have had no imperfection in our record." (Morm. 9:33.) The King James Version has marvelously retained much of the poetic beauty found in the Hebrew text of Isaiah's writings.

Keys that Must Be Developed

Although the previous three golden keys may be applied with immediate results, the book of Isaiah cannot be fully understood without five additional keys. These five major keys take considerable development, but unlock the doors to the flood of light and knowledge found in the book of Isaiah. These five grand keys are:
1. Have a knowledge of the gospel and God's dealings with his people.

2. Have the spirit of prophecy in reading.
3. Be aware of Isaiah's doctrinal themes.
4. Be familiar with the customs of, and manner of prophesying among, the Jews.
5. Be engaged in continuous and conscientious study.

The three golden keys of immediate application are actually derived from the above five major keys.

If one does not hesitate to tackle the problem of understanding Isaiah, but approaches it with a positive attitude, he will be pleasantly surprised to find that these five keys will come naturally and will gradually increase his ability to use them as diligent reading continues. The following explanation of these keys may be helpful:

1. *Have a knowledge of the gospel and God's dealings with his people.* This grand key includes: (1) a knowledge of the restoration; (2) familiarity with the covenant, the covenant people, and their destiny; (3) knowledge of the purpose of the Lord concerning the nations of the earth in the last days; and (4) knowledge and use of other scriptures.

Knowledge Unique to the Restoration

Since Isaiah told of the restoration in the last days and how various elements of the restoration would come to pass, most people would not understand these prophecies unless they were familiar with the latter-day restoration itself. Therefore, only members of the Church who are familiar with the events, principles, functions, and activities of the Church can understand Isaiah's great, panoramic visions. For example, if one did not understand how missionaries were sent out during the first century and a half of the latter-day Church, he would not recognize Isaiah's injunction, "Go, ye swift messengers, to a nation scattered and peeled." (Isa. 18:2.)

The coming forth of the Book of Mormon, depicted in Isaiah chapter 29, is another scene in Isaiah's panorama of the last days only understood by those who know the history of the Book of Mormon:

> And the vision of all is become unto you as the words of a book that is sealed, which men deliver to one that is learned, saying, Read this, I pray

> thee: and he saith, I cannot; for it is sealed: And the book is delivered to him that is not learned, saying, Read this, I pray thee: and he saith, I am not learned . . . Therefore, behold, I will proceed to do a marvellous work among this people, even a marvellous work and a wonder: for the wisdom of their wise men shall perish, and the understanding of their prudent men shall be hid. (Isa. 29:11-12, 14.)

Unless one is familiar with the transplanting of the Church to the Rocky Mountains, he cannot appreciate Isaiah's prophecies:

> And it shall come to pass in the last days, that the mountain of the Lord's house shall be established in the top of the mountains, and shall be exalted above the hills; and all nations shall flow unto it. (Isa. 2:2.)

> All ye inhabitants of the world, and dwellers on the earth, see ye, when he lifteth up an ensign on the mountains; and when he bloweth a trumpet, hear ye. (Isa. 18:3.)

> And I will bring forth a seed out of Jacob, and out of Judah an inheritor of my mountains: and mine elect shall inherit it, and my servants shall dwell there. (Isa. 65:9.)

One needs to be familiar with the special mission of the two latter-day prophets and what happens to them (see Bruce R. McConkie, *Mormon Doctrine*, p. 733) to understand Isaiah's prophecy concerning Jerusalem:

> There is none to guide her among all the sons whom she hath brought forth; neither is there any that taketh her by the hand of all the sons that she hath brought up.
> These two things [sons] are come unto thee; who shall be sorry for thee? desolation, and destruction, and the famine, and the sword: by whom shall I comfort thee?
> Thy sons (these two) have fainted, they lie at the head of all the streets, as a wild bull in a net: they are full of the fury of the Lord, the rebuke of thy God. (Isa. 51:18-20; see Joseph Smith Translation.)

In many passages, Isaiah assumes that those to whom he is speaking have received many of the sacred ordinances. For example, chapter 22 of Isaiah cannot be fully understood unless one is familiar with the temple endowments and covenants:

> And I will fasten him as a nail in a sure place; and he shall be for a glorious throne to his father's house. . . . In that day, saith the Lord of hosts, shall the nail that is fastened in the sure place be removed, and be cut down, and fall; and the burden that was upon it shall be cut off: for the Lord hath spoken it. (Isa. 22:23, 25.)

Elder Bruce R. McConkie stated that the book of Isaiah was written to people who already know that Jesus is the Christ and understand the principle of the Atonement and works necessary to inherit the celestial kingdom. (*Ensign,* Oct. 1973, p. 80.)

Knowledge of the Plan of Salvation

One reading the book of Isaiah needs to understand the basic doctrines concerning the plan of salvation and God's dealings with his people. Alert reading will reveal the message of the restored gospel throughout Isaiah's prophecies. Examples of topics and passages only understood by those familiar with God's plan of salvation are:

1. Premortal events in heaven.

> How art thou fallen from heaven, O Lucifer, son of the morning! how art thou cut down to the ground, which didst weaken the nations! For thou hast said in thine heart, I will ascend into heaven, I will exalt my throne above the stars of God: I will sit also upon the mount of the congregation, in the sides of the north: I will ascend above the heights of the clouds; I will be like the most High. Yet thou shalt be brought down to hell, to the sides of the pit. (Isa. 14:12-15.)

2. Christ's visit to the spirit world.

> And they shall be gathered together, as prisoners are gathered in the pit, and shall be shut up in the prison, and after many days shall they be visited. (Isa. 24:22.)

> To open blind eyes, to bring out the prisoners from the prison, and them that sit in darkness out of the prison house. (Isa. 42:7.)

3. Events of the Restoration.

> And he will lift up an ensign to the nations from far, and will hiss unto them from the end of the earth: and, behold, they shall come with speed swiftly. (Isa. 5:26.)

And it shall come to pass in the last days, that the mountain of the Lord's house shall be established in the top of the mountains, and shall be exalted above the hills; and all nations shall flow unto it. And many people shall go and say, Come ye, and let us go up to the mountain of the Lord, to the house of the God of Jacob; and he will teach us of his ways, and we will walk in his paths: for out of Zion shall go forth the law, and the word of the Lord from Jerusalem. (Isa. 2:2-3.)

One of the keys to understanding the scriptures is to use other scriptures. One may ask, "What do other scriptures say about this topic or passage?" Isaiah is quoted extensively in the Book of Mormon and the Bible. The more perfect translation of Isaiah's writings in the Book of Mormon helps one to understand Isaiah. A classical example is Isaiah 2:9: "And the mean man boweth down and the great man humbleth himself: therefore forgive them not." (Isa. 2:9.) Since this is misleading doctrine, it is difficult to understand. The Book of Mormon adds the word *not,* making the translation both correct and understandable: "And the mean man boweth *not* down, and the great man humbleth himself *not,* therefore forgive him not." (2 Ne. 12:9; italics added.) Elder Bruce R. McConkie stated that the Book of Mormon is the world's greatest commentary on the book of Isaiah. (*Ensign*, Oct. 1973, p. 81.)

Isaiah is quoted in the New Testament by the Savior, the Apostle Paul, Peter, and others. Matthew 12:17-21 helps us to realize that Isaiah 42:1-3 is a prophecy concerning the Savior:

Matthew 12:17-21	Isaiah 42:1-3
That it might be fulfilled which was spoken by Esaias the prophet, saying, Behold my servant, whom I have chosen; my beloved, in whom my soul is well pleased: I will put my spirit upon him, and he shall shew judgment to the Gentiles. He shall not strive, nor cry; neither shall any man hear his voice in the streets. A bruised reed shall he not break, and smoking flax shall he not quench, till he send forth judgment unto victory. And in his name shall the Gentiles trust.	Behold my servant, whom I uphold; mine elect, in whom my soul delighteth; I have put my spirit upon him: he shall bring forth judgment to the Gentiles. He shall not cry, nor lift up, nor cause his voice to be heard in the street. A bruised reed shall he not break, and the smoking flax shall he not quench: he shall bring forth judgment unto truth.

The fact that these two passages differ in wording could present a slight problem. Some investigators have thought that when the Book of Mormon quotes biblical passages, the quotes should be verbatim. Others have thought that there should be very little or no similarity, and that too much similarity is somehow evidence that the Book of Mormon is not true. However, when one considers that the origin of the texts are from two different languages and translations, he must expect such changes in wording. The Isaiah text in the Bible came down through various transcriptions and abridgments from the Hebrew text. The version in Matthew came from the Greek text, which in turn quotes a Hebrew text. These slight differences actually serve as evidence that quotations in the Book of Mormon can also be expected to be similar, but with slight variations.

The Doctrine and Covenants provides additional unique interpretations of the words of Isaiah. When we read a passage in the Doctrine and Covenants, we tend to feel more comfortable with it and understand it because we interpret it in the setting of our own day. But that same passage found in Isaiah is not generally understood. For example, is the following passage from Isaiah or the Doctrine and Covenants?

> In all their afflictions he was afflicted. And the angel of his presence saved them; and in his love, and in his pity, he redeemed them, and bore them, and carried them all the days of old.

If this passage were from Isaiah, we would tend to ask, "What specifically is it about? Does it refer to those in Isaiah's day, in Jesus' day, our day, or some other?" But if the passage is from the Doctrine and Covenants we tend to try to interpret it in some way as applying to us. We would be apt to read this passage in the Doctrine and Covenants as referring to the atonement of Christ, and therefore say that it applies to those of us in the everlasting covenant.

This passage is found both in Doctrine and Covenants 133:53 and Isaiah 63:9. In fact, if one were to read all of Isaiah 63 and then Doctrine and Covenants 133:58-63, he might be surprised at how much more meaningful these verses are in the Doctrine and Covenants. It might be helpful to pretend to be reading the Doctrine and Covenants when reading the book of Isaiah.

The Doctrine and Covenants is a tool for interpreting Isaiah's words in still other ways. For example, Doctrine and Covenants 113 is especially helpful for interpreting chapters 11 and 52 of Isaiah. From this section we know that Isaiah was prophesying of the coming of the Savior, in addition to other latter-day events:

Isaiah 11:1-2	*Doctrine and Covenants 113:1-4*
And there shall come forth a rod out of the stem of Jesse, and a Branch shall grow out of his roots: And the spirit of the Lord shall rest upon him, the spirit of wisdom and understanding, the spirit of counsel and might, the spirit of knowledge and of the fear of the Lord;	Who is the Stem of Jesse spoken of in the 1st, 2d, 3d, 4th, and 5th verses of the 11th chapter of Isaiah? Verily thus saith the Lord: It is Christ. What is the rod spoken of in the first verse of the 11th chapter of Isaiah, that should come out of the Stem of Jesse? Behold, thus saith the Lord: It is a servant in the hands of Christ, who is partly a descendant of Jesse as well as of Ephraim, or of the house of Joseph, on whom there is laid much power.

Numerous phrases in the book of Isaiah are also found in the Doctrine and Covenants. The Doctrine and Covenants passages help us to understand the language of Isaiah. Phrases common to various prophets and ages are sometimes referred to as "the language of [the] fathers." (Mosiah 1:2.)

Who are the fathers (his fathers [1 Ne. 5:14], their fathers [1 Ne. 15:14], our fathers [1 Ne. 3:19], your fathers [D&C 45:16]) referred to in the scriptures? These fathers are the righteous patriarchs, the holy prophets. Thus, the language of the fathers is simply the language of the prophets, or the word of the Lord through the prophets. Their language is a gospel language. There are certain phrases that have meaning only to those who know the gospel. For example, the phrases *Eternal life, Eternal punishment,* and *Endless torment* have specific meanings to the Saints that are not understood by nonmembers. Even *exaltation, to be lifted up,* and *damnation* have entirely different meanings to members of the Church than to the rest of the world. The Lord has said:

> Nevertheless, it is not written that there shall be no end to this torment, but it is written *endless torment.*
> Again, it is written *eternal damnation;* wherefore it is more express than other scriptures, that it might work upon the hearts of the children of men, altogether for my name's glory.

Wherefore, I will explain unto you this mystery, for it is meet unto you
to know even as mine apostles. (D&C 19:6-8.)

These specific gospel phrases in the language of the fathers are
given for us to know, "even as mine apostles," for our salvation,
"that you may enter into my rest." (D&C 19:8-9.) This is a marvelous promise to those who diligently seek to know the language
of the fathers. The language of the fathers is given "that it might
work upon the hearts of the children of men" for the fulfillment
of this marvelous promise. (D&C 19:7.)

There are many phrases having specific meaning in the language of the fathers that are not understood by the world. For example, one day three men came to my office to try to prove that
Brigham Young taught the so-called Adam-God theory. One of
the men was a local sectarian minister, one was an apostate, and
one was an immigrant who spent much of his time fighting against
the Church. They were surprised to find that I was thoroughly
familiar with the dozen quotations they had taken from the
Journal of Discourses. In fact, I had some they did not have that
shed a much different light on the subject. These men then wanted
to know why their quotations seemed to say something different
than what I insisted Brigham Young taught. I found that these
men could not even understand me, let alone Brigham Young.
They could not be made to understand a number of phrases from
the language of the fathers. Those who do not have the Holy
Ghost cannot understand things of the Spirit; therefore, they
cannot understand the language of the fathers.

Another example is the mistranslation made by biblical translators who did not know the meaning of *Eternity* in the third
chapter of Ecclesiastes. This special use of *Eternity* in the language
of the fathers has reference to God or the things of God. (D&C
19:6-13.) The mistranslation is in the eleventh verse:

> I have seen the travail, which God hath given to the sons of men to be
> exercised in it. He hath made every thing beautiful in his time: also he hath
> set *the world in their heart, so that* no man can find out the work that God
> maketh from the beginning to the end. (Eccl. 3:10-11; italics added.)

Now try reading the eleventh verse, substituting the following
phrase for the phrase in italics:

> Eternity (God) in their heart, without which...

The verse as it is in the Bible is not pure truth and light. It also contradicts Isaiah's words, "Remember the former things of old: for I am God, and there is none else; I am God, and there is none like me, Declaring the end from the beginning, and from ancient times the things that are not yet done." (Isa. 46:9-10.) Jacob, in the Book of Mormon, taught the true concept: "And no man knoweth of his ways save it be revealed unto him; wherefore, brethren, despise not the revelations of God." (Jacob 4:8.) The Hebrew word *olam* was misinterpreted in Ecclesiastes 3:11 to read "the world," but more accurately means *eternity*.

There are many phrases throughout the standard works that can be compared to increase our understanding as they work upon our hearts. For example, comparing the phrases common to both the Doctrine and Covenants and the forty-ninth chapter of Isaiah, one is able to see that at least three different servants are referred to within the first seven verses of Isaiah 49. These servants include the house of Israel (49:3), the Savior (49:1-2, 4-9), and a latter-day prophet-servant who gathers in the house of Israel and who is a light unto the Gentiles (49:4-6). Isaiah 49:1 may be compared with Doctrine and Covenants 1:1, 1:17, 127:2, and so on. The language of the fathers is found in both texts:

Isaiah	*Doctrine and Covenants*
Listen, O isles, unto me; and hearken, ye people, from afar. (Isa. 49:1.)	Hearken, O ye people of my church, saith the voice of him who dwells on high, and whose eyes are upon all men; yea, verily I say: Hearken ye people from afar; and ye that are upon the islands of the sea, listen together. (D&C 1:1.)
And he hath made my mouth like a sharp sword; in the shadow of his hand hath he hid me, and made me a polished shaft; in his quiver hath he hid me; (Isa. 49:2.)	Behold, I am God; give heed unto my word, which is quick and powerful, sharper than a two-edged sword, to the dividing asunder of both joints and marrow; therefore give heed unto my words. (D&C 6:2.)
And he said, It is a light thing that thou shouldest be my servant to raise up the tribes of Jacob, and to restore the preserved of Israel: I will also give thee for a light to the Gentiles, that thou mayest be my salvation unto the end of the earth. (Isa. 49:6.)	Therefore, blessed are ye if ye continue in my goodness, a light unto the Gentiles, and through this priesthood, a savior unto my people Israel. The Lord hath said it. Amen. (D&C 86:11.)

We can also note the similarity, the familiar spirit, in the language of the prophets between Isaiah 34 and the Doctrine and Covenants:

Isaiah	*Doctrine and Covenantss*
For the indignation of the Lord is upon all nations, and his fury upon all their armies: he hath utterly destroyed them, he hath delivered them to the slaughter. (Isa. 34:2.)	Mine indignation is soon to be poured out without measure upon all nations; and this will I do when the cup of their iniquity is full. (D&C 101:11.)
For my sword shall be bathed in heaven: behold, it shall come down upon Idumea, and upon the people of my curse, to judgment. (Isa. 34:5.)	For a desolating scourge shall go forth among the inhabitants of the earth, and shall continue to be poured out from time to time, if they repent not, until the earth is empty, and the inhabitants thereof are consumed away and utterly destroyed by the brightness of my coming. (D&C 5:19.)
...it shall come down upon Idumea, ...(Isa. 34:5.)	
	And the anger of the Lord is kindled, and his sword is bathed in heaven, and it shall fall upon the inhabitants of the earth. (D&C 1:13.)
	And also the Lord shall have power over his saints, and shall reign in their midst, and shall come down in judgment upon Idumea, or the world. (D&C 1:36.)

For other examples, Isaiah 58:7 can be compared with D&C 104:18, Isaiah 62:12 with D&C 98, and Isaiah 63:2-3 with D&C 133:45 and 51.

Isaiah stated that the Book of Mormon would be "as of one that hath a familiar spirit, out of the ground." (Isa. 29:4.) The language in the Doctrine and Covenants has just as familiar a spirit to the words of Isaiah as does the Book of Mormon.

Although some prophets spoke different languages in different periods of time and in different nations than others, there were certain phrases in each particular language that represented a gospel concept common to the language of the fathers.

Elder Bruce R. McConkie stated:

It truly takes revelation to understand revelation, and what is more natural than to find the Lord Jehovah, who revealed his truths anciently, revealing the same eternal verities today and so tying his ancient and modern words together, that we may be blessed by our knowledge of what he has said in all ages. (*Ensign*, Oct. 1973, p. 81.)

Modern variant translations of the Bible often lose the real meaning of the passages because they change the language of the fathers. In this respect, the Prophet Joseph's work on the Bible was more of a restoration than a translation.

Deep Doctrines

From the perspective of the revealed gospel, it is easy to see why Elder McConkie stated:

No one, absolutely no one, in this age and dispensation has or does or can understand the writings of Isaiah until he first learns and believes what God has revealed by the mouths of his Nephite witnesses as these truths are found in that volume of holy writ. (*Ensign*, Oct. 1973, p. 81.)

Isaiah must have foreseen our predicament in attempting to understand his words, when he exclaimed:

Whom shall he teach knowledge?
And whom shall he make to understand doctrine?
Those who are weaned from milk,
Those who are drawn from the breasts. (Isa. 28:9.)

Thus, Isaiah himself tells us that only those who have a good foundation in the gospel principles can hope to be taught knowledge and understand the deeper doctrines found in his words. The book of Isaiah is for those who can endure meat. Paul uses this same metaphor: "I have fed you with milk, and not with meat: for hitherto ye were not able to bear it, neither yet now are ye able." (1 Cor. 3:2.)

Approaching the book of Isaiah with the gospel background and an understanding of the scriptures will allow our souls to delight in Isaiah's words. The rest of the world remains in darkness, not knowing the light, until they can accept the gospel of Christ:

The people that walked in darkness have seen a great light: they that dwell in the land of the shadow of death, upon them hath the light shined. Thou hast multiplied the nation, and increased the joy to him: they joy before thee according to the joy in harvest, and as men rejoice when they divide the spoil. (Isa. 9:2-3, Joseph Smith Translation.)

Some years ago in New Zealand during a sectarian revival meeting, a preacher was expounding about salvation. A Mormon missionary in the audience spoke up saying, "Salvation without exaltation is damnation." The perplexed preacher stood dumbfounded for a few moments and then replied, "Maybe that Mormon missionary knows what he said, but I don't." They both had spoken the truth. There are many gospel terms not understood by the sectarian world. Sanctification through the cleansing power of the Holy Ghost is only understood by Latter-day Saints who are familiar with their doctrine. The sectarian world could not appreciate Isaiah's glorious scene depicting the faithful Latter-day Saints:

Lift ye up a banner upon the high mountain,
Exalt the voice unto them,
Shake the hand,
That they may go into the gates of the nobles.
I have commanded my sanctified ones,
I have also called my mighty ones for mine anger,
Even them that rejoice in my highness. (Isa. 13:2-3.)

One needs more than mere baptism to fully appreciate the meaning of Isaiah 57:15. In addition, one must have a broken heart and a contrite spirit through the Holy Ghost:

For thus saith the high and lofty One
That inhabiteth eternity, whose name is Holy;
I dwell in the high and holy place,
With him also that is of a contrite and humble spirit,
To revive the spirit of the humble,
And to revive the heart of the contrite ones. (Isa. 57:15.)

The more one grows in the gospel principles, understanding the doctrine "precept upon precept and line upon line" (Isa. 28:9-10), the more the words of Isaiah penetrate and thrill him.

2. *Have the spirit of prophecy in reading.* In one sense, this is perhaps the most important key of all. Any other key must be used in conjunction with this one. The spirit of prophecy is the spirit of revelation. It takes revelation to understand revelation. Peter stated, "Knowing this first, that no prophecy of the scriptures is of any private interpretation. For the prophecy came not in old time by the will of man: but holy men of God spake as they were moved by the Holy Ghost." (2 Pet. 1:20-21.)

The Apostle Paul warned that all things pertaining to God can only be understood by the revelations of the Spirit: "For what man knoweth the things of man, save the spirit of man which is in him? even so the things of God knoweth no man, but the spirit of God." (1 Cor. 2:11.) It is therefore important to seek the Holy Ghost each time one expects to read and understand the words of Isaiah.

John informs us that "the testimony of Jesus is the spirit of prophecy." (Rev. 19:10.) Thus, key two is closely related to key one (knowledge of the gospel), since a person must have a testimony of Jesus to have the spirit of prophecy. Conversely, if one does not have the spirit of prophecy, one does not have a true testimony of Jesus, though he might think he does.

Nephi stated that the words of Isaiah are "plain unto all those that are filled with the spirit of prophecy." (2 Ne. 25:4.) In reading this passage after skimming over the words of Isaiah in the Book of Mormon, I would subconsciously think, "I must not be *filled* with the spirit of prophecy." However, this was not the case. I had a testimony of Jesus, and therefore the spirit of prophecy. The *real* problem was that I did not try to *use* the spirit of prophecy. Although one might have a key to open a door, trying to open the locked door without using the key does him little good. One needs to diligently search the words of Isaiah as the Savior commanded (3 Ne. 23:1), by *applying* the testimony of Jesus. With each application, the light becomes brighter in the seeking soul. When Laman and Lemuel could not understand their father's revelations, Nephi asked them, "Have ye inquired of the Lord?" (1 Ne. 15:8.) The promise given by Nephi is: "For he that diligently seeketh shall find; and the mysteries of God shall be unfolded unto them, by the power of the Holy Ghost." (1 Ne. 10:19.)

The more one applies this tool, the more skillful he becomes at using it, the sharper the tool becomes for cutting away the deadwood that camouflages understanding, and the more joyous the words of Isaiah become.

A few years ago a seminary student had accepted a challenge given in class to inquire of the Lord. Several days later he returned to class, exclaiming, "It works! It works!" The seminary teacher asked the student if inspiration and understanding came easily, or if the student had to work at it. The student replied that it took lots of effort, but that it really worked. The more he applied himself, the greater understanding he obtained. The teacher made the mental note, "Now I won't have to worry about that student anymore. He's headed in the right direction." A few months later, the teacher observed that he had been mistaken. The student was having problems with the school administration, his family, the ward leaders, and seminary. The teacher quizzed him and found to his disappointment that the student had stopped trying. He had lost his pearl of great price. The spirit of understanding had left when he traded it for some thrills of the world. "And that wicked one cometh and taketh away light and truth, through disobedience, from the children of men, and because of the tradition of their fathers." (D&C 93:39.)

It is amusing to read some of the commentaries on Isaiah by biblical scholars to see how far amiss their interpretations are, though the authors are very sincere in their commentary. For example, a commentary on Isaiah 2:2, "the Lord's house shall be established in the top of the mountains," says that this verse refers to Jerusalem. Since Jerusalem and Mount Olivet are near sea level and much lower than the few mountains in the Holy Land, especially compared to Mount Herman (9,400 ft.) on the north, this commentary claims: "Mount Zion is to be physically raised, and to become fixed at the head of the lower mountains, which radiate as it were, in all directions from it." (T. K. Cheyne, *Prophecies of Isaiah*, p. 16.)

One reason that the classical Hebrew in the Old Testament is best understood by reading with feeling is that revelation comes partly by way of feeling, as Spirit speaks to spirit. Since the Old Testament prophets wrote and spoke by the Spirit, their words must be understood by the Spirit. Therefore, reading by trying to gain a feeling for what is being said helps one to be sensitive to the Spirit's promptings.

3. *Be aware of Isaiah's doctrinal themes.* Isaiah's prophecies are like a beautiful flower garden—they have enough repetition to be fully impressive, yet enough variety to be intriguing. There are quite a number of doctrinal themes in his prophecies and messages. A knowledge of the gospel helps considerably in recognizing and understanding Isaiah's doctrinal themes.

Isaiah himself gives us a clue to the major theme of his prophecies: "Behold, I and the children whom the Lord hath given me are for signs and for wonders in Israel from the Lord of Hosts, which dwelleth in mount Zion." (Isa. 8:18.) Isaiah then proceeds to expand upon these "signs and wonders" that Isaiah and his sons represent. For example, in 9:2 he states, "The people that walked in darkness have seen a great light." And in 9:6 he states, "For unto us a child is born, unto us a son is given: and the government shall be upon his shoulder: and his name shall be called Wonderful, Counseller, The mighty God, The everlasting Father, The Prince of Peace." Thus, Isaiah, as all prophets, points us to the great light and life of the Son of God. As one becomes more familiar with the life of Isaiah and his prophecies, one is impressed with the parallel of Isaiah's life to that of the Savior.

Isaiah's name and the names of his children bear the underlying message of the book of Isaiah. Isaiah's name means "Jehovah is salvation," or "Jehovah is the savior," or "Jehovah is the Redeemer." The name of his son Mahershalalhashbaz means "make speed the spoil, hasten the prey." The name of Isaiah's other son, Sherajashub, means "the remnant shall return." These are the three major messages of Isaiah to the house of Israel:

1. True hope and salvation is only in the Lord.
2. Since you will not repent, you soon shall be destroyed and scattered.
3. Only a remnant shall be left to return unto the Lord in the last days.

Isaiah's constant message was for all people to come unto the Lord and accept His redemptive power. Both personal and national salvation depended upon trust in the Lord. This is the literal meaning of Isaiah's name. His message to the kings of his day consisted of warnings for them to trust in the Lord, whether in time of peace or war. In time of war, he warned them that putting their trust in anything but the Lord was like putting their trust in a sinking ship. The results of such misplaced trust would only be destruction:

> Say ye not, A confederacy, to all them to whom this people shall say, A confederacy; neither fear ye their fear, nor be afraid. Sanctify the Lord of hosts himself; and let him be your fear, and let him be your dread. And he shall be for a sanctuary; but for a stone of stumbling and for a rock of offence to both the houses of Israel, for a gin and for a snare to the inhabitants of Jerusalem. And many among them shall stumble, and fall, and be broken, and be snared, and be taken. (Isa. 8:12-15.)

Instead of "let him be your fear, and... your dread," we might want to read, "let him be in place of your fear, and... in place of your dread."

The three themes inherent in the meaning of the names of Isaiah and his two sons become very obvious to the watchful eye.

Many prophecies are of multiple meanings and fulfillments. The basic remnant theme of Isaiah is that there will be those of the house of Israel in the last days who do return to the gospel and live the covenants. A second meaning of the returning remnant is that remnants of the house of Israel will return to Jerusalem. Understanding these and other related concepts of the remnant, one can realize that the return of the Jews from Babylon to Jerusalem and the rebuilding of the temple in the days of kings Cyrus and Darius was only a partial and limited fulfillment of the remnant prophecies. The following prophecy is definitely of the latter-day remnant in their righteous state:

> And the light of Israel shall be for a fire, and his Holy One for a flame: and it shall burn and devour his thorns and his briers in one day; And shall consume the glory of his forest, and of his fruitful field, both soul and body: and they shall be as when a standardbearer fainteth. And the rest of the trees of his forest shall be few, that a child may write them.
>
> And it shall come to pass in that day, that the remnant of Israel, and such as are escaped of the house of Jacob, shall no more again stay upon him that smote them; but shall stay upon the Lord, the Holy One of Israel, in truth. The remnant shall return, even the remnant of Jacob, unto the mighty God. (Isa. 10:17-21.)

Because the remnant was to come forth in the last days, the house of Israel was not totally destroyed, but instead scattered as

Isaiah predicted: "Except the Lord of hosts had left unto us a very small remnant, we should have been as Sodom, and we should have been like unto Gomorrah." (Isa. 1:9.)

This is also evidence that even in their wicked state, a few members of the remnant in Isaiah's days believed the prophets. One of the apocryphal books of the Bible is the book of Tobit. This book is about a man by the name of Tobit who lived during Isaiah's lifetime. Tobit was of the tribe of Naphtali, and had been led captive from Galilee to Nineveh by the Assyrians. According to this account, Tobit was a righteous man, and at the end of his life he called his son Tobias unto him and told him to leave Nineveh, because this wicked city in Assyria was prophesied by Jonas to be destroyed if they did not repent. Tobit warned his son Tobias not to flee to Jerusalem because of its wickedness and the destruction prophesied by Isaiah. He told him to go to Media instead, that he might avoid the destructions. By obeying this prophecy, Tobias helped to scatter a remnant:

> Go into Media, my son, for I surely believe those things which Jonas the prophet spake of Nineve, that it shall be overthrown; and that for a time peace shall rather be in Media; and that our brethren shall lie scattered in the earth from that good land: and Jerusalem shall be desolate, and the house of God in it shall be burned, and shall be desolate for a time; And that again God will have mercy on them, and bring them again into the land, where they shall build a temple, but not like to the first, until the time of that age be fulfilled; and afterward they shall return from all places of their captivity, and build up Jerusalem gloriously, and the house of God shall be built in it for ever with a glorious building, as the prophets have spoken thereof. (Tobit 14:4-5.)

These prophecies contain some of the details of Isaiah's prophecies concerning the destruction, scattering, and restoration of the house of Israel. Isaiah's theme of the remnant has far-reaching implications, as do many of his other themes.

Themes from the Book of Isaiah

Theme	Reference
1. Remnant to return	1:9; 2:3; 4:3; 10:20-22; 11:16; 15:9; 18:7; 37:32; 44:28.

2.	Messianic prophecy related to Christ's first coming	1:18; 7:14-15; 9:2-7; 11:1-5; 6:9-10; 7:10-16; 8:17-18; 16:4-5; 22:21-25; 25:8; 28:16; 32:1-4; 41:11; 41:27; 42:1-8, 16; 45:20-25; parts of 49:1-13; 50:4-7; 52:3-15; 53; 61:1-3; 63:9; 66:7.
3.	Messianic prophecy related to the Second Coming	2:10-21; 4:4; 9:18-19; 10:16-34; 11:4-5, 14-16; 13:6-22; 24:6-23; 25-26; 30:27-33; 31:9; 33:11-17; 34; 40; 60:19-22; 61; 63-64.
4.	The latter-day restoration	2:2-3; 5:26-30; 11:10-14; 14:1-3; 18; 24:13-16; 26:15-18; 28:5, 9-14; 29; 32:15-20; 33: 4-6; 41; 43; 44; 49:1-6, 22; 54; 60-61.
5.	The Gathering	2:2-3; 10:22; 11:11; 14:1-2; 18; 24:13; 32: 19-20; 33:4; 43:5-9; 45:20-25; 49:5-6, 22-26; 51:11; 65:8-9; 66:18-21.
6.	The Millennium	2:4, 17-19; 4; 11:6-9; 12; 19:19-25; 25-28; 30; 33:20-24; 35; 43:19-21; 54:11-14; 55:12-13; 65:17-25; 66:20-24.
7.	Warning to Latter-day Saints	2:19; 3-4; 13:1-5; 26:17-21; 28; 32:9-15; 56-60; 65-66.
8.	Care for the poor and needy	1:17, 23; 3:14-15; 9:17; 10:2; 11:14; 14:30, 32; 25:4; 26:6; 29:19; 32:7; 41:17; 58:6-7; 66:2.
9.	Warnings to the wicked	1; 2:10-22; 3-5; 9-10; 14-17; 19; 21-24; 28; 34; 46-48; 56; 65-66.
10.	Promises of peace and joy to the faithful	25-27; 48:18; 54:10, 13; 55:12; 57:1-2, 19; 60:15; 61:10-11; 65:14, 18-19; 66:5, 10-14 (over 100 references to this concept in Isaiah).
11.	Apostasy	1; 3; 5; 9:20-21; 10; 14; 21-24; 28; 30; 33:1-9; 47; 48:1-8; 55-59; 65:1-16; 66:15-18.
12.	Scattering of Israel	2:2-5; 5:5-7, 13; 8:15; 16:4; 30:16-17; 33:3; 61:9.
13.	The everlasting covenant	24:5; 33:8; 42:6; 54:10; 55:3; 56:4, 6; 61:8.

Watching for Isaiah's major themes is often necessary in studying the book of Isaiah, since these themes are sometimes couched in metaphors, parables, and historical events that otherwise camouflage the message given. In addition, these themes are expressed in the language of the fathers, the "tongue of angels'' or power of the Holy Ghost. (2 Ne. 31:13.) Members of the Church under the influence of the Holy Ghost generally talk about the same themes as did Isaiah. An excellent example of a modern Church member expressing these themes in the language of the fathers is Mary Fielding Smith.

After having left England, Mary Fielding and her sister Mercy went to Canada, where their brother Joseph Fielding and his wife resided. Joseph, having accepted the gospel, introduced it to his two sisters, who likewise joined the Church. From the beginning of Mary's new life as a member, she was thrust into the midst of afflictions and persecutions that came initially from apostate members of the Church in Kirtland, Ohio. During these initial trials to the Church and persecutions heaped upon Joseph Smith by would-be leaders of the Church who would not humble themselves and repent, Mary Fielding also found her life threatened by these apostate forces of the adversary. As the years passed, such afflictions became common, almost habitual, in Mary's life. The martyrdom of her husband, Hyrum Smith, was no exception, but continued in the course for which Mary Fielding had been adequately prepared through her previous paths of afflictions. By the time Mary Fielding came West across the plains with her children, she had already resigned herself to such ordeals, realizing their necessity and purpose. These excerpts from some of Mary's letters parallel Isaiah's messages to the remnant in the last days:

Mary Fielding	
Peace amid Tribulations	*Isaiah*
I do thank my Heavenly Father for the comfort and peace of mind I now enjoy in the midst of all the confusion and	Lord, thou wilt ordain peace for us: for thou also has wrought all our works in us. (Isa. 26:12.)
	From the uttermost part of the earth have we heard songs, even glory to the righteous. (Isa. 24:16.)
perplexity and raging of the devil against the work of God in this place, for although there is a great number of faithful, precious souls, yea, the salt of the earth, yet it may be truly called a place where Satan has his seat;	Therefore hell hath enlarged herself, and opened her mouth without measure: and their glory, and their multitude, and their pomp, and he that rejoiceth, shall descend into it. (Isa. 5:14.)

He is frequently stirring up some of the people to strife and contention and dissatisfaction with things they do not understand.

The city of confusion is broken down: every house is shut up, that no man may come in. . . . But I said, My leanness, my leanness, woe unto me! the treacherous dealers have dealt treacherously; yea, the treacherous dealers have dealt very treacherously. (Isa. 24:10, 16.)

We are not yet able to tell where it will end.

For yet a very little while, and the indignation shall cease, and mine anger in their destruction. (Isa. 10:25.)

I have been made to tremble and quake before the Lord and to call upon Him with all my heart almost day and night, as many others have done of late.

When thus it shall be in the midst of the land among the people, there shall be as the shaking of an olive tree, and as the gleaning grapes when the vintage is done. (Isa. 24:13.)

Fear, and the pit, and the snare, are upon thee, O inhabitant of the earth. (Isa. 24:17.)

Purpose of Suffering

I feel more and more convinced that it is through suffering that we are to be made perfect, and I have already found it to have the effect of driving me nearer to the Lord and so suffering has become a great blessing to me.

In all their affliction he was afflicted, and the angel of his presence saved them: in his love and in his pity he redeemed them; and he bare them, and carried them all the days of old. (Isa. 63:9.)

. . . Fear not: for I have redeemed thee, I have called thee by thy name; thou art mine. (Isa. 43:1.)

I have sometimes of late been so filled with the love of God, and felt such essence of his favor as has made me rejoice abundantly indeed. My heavenly Father has been very gracious unto me both temporally and spiritually.

I have commanded my sanctified ones, I have also called my mighty ones . . . even them that rejoice in my highness. (Isa. 13:3.)

They shall lift up their voice, they shall sing for the majesty of the Lord, they shall cry aloud from the sea. (Isa. 24:14.)

When thou passest through the waters, I will be with thee; and through the rivers, they shall not overflow thee: when thou walkest through the fire, thou shalt not be burned; neither shall the flame kindle upon thee. (Isa. 43:2.)

Experiencing the Atonement

So many important things have transpired, and so great have been my afflictions, etc., that I know not where to begin; but I can say, hitherto has the Lord preserved me, and I am still among the living to praise him, as I do today. I have, to be sure, been called to drink of the bitter cup; but you know my beloved brother, this makes the sweet sweeter.

Mind Stayed upon God

I feel but little concern about where I am, if I can keep my mind staid upon God; for, you know in this there is perfect peace.

I believe the Lord is overruling all things for our good. I suppose our enemies look upon us with astonishment and disappointment.... Yet I do not feel in the least discouraged;

Promise of a Glorious Reward

now though my sister and I are here together in a strange land, we have been enabled to rejoice, in the midst of our privations and persecutions, that we were counted worthy to suffer these things, so that we may, with the ancient saints who suffered in like manner, inherit the same glorious reward.

Therefore shall the strong people glorify thee, the city of the terrible nations shall fear thee. For thou hast been a strength to the poor, a strength to the needy in his distress, a refuge from the storm, a shadow from the heat, when the blast of the terrible ones is as a storm against the wall.... And in this mountain shall the Lord of hosts make unto all people a feast of fat things, a feast of wines on the lees, of fat things full of marrow, of wines on the lees well refined. (Isa. 25:3-4,6.)

He will swallow up death in victory; and the Lord God will wipe away tears from off all faces; and the rebuke of his people shall he take away from off all the earth: for the Lord hath spoken it. And it shall be said in that day, Lo, this is our God; we have waited for him, and he will save us: this is the Lord; we have waited for him, we will be glad and rejoice in his salvation. (Isa. 25:8-9.)

Thou wilt keep him in perfect peace, whose mind is stayed on thee: because he trusteth in thee. (Isa. 26:3.)

And my people shall dwell in a peaceable habitation, and in sure dwellings, and in quiet resting places. (Isa. 32:18.)

When thou criest, let thy companies deliver thee; but the wind shall carry them all away; vanity shall take them: but he that putteth his trust in me shall possess the land, and shall inherit my holy mountain. (Isa. 57:13.)

And if children, then heirs; heirs of God, and joint-heirs with Christ; if so be that we suffer with him, that we may be also glorified together. (Romans 8:17.)

If it had not been for this hope, I should have sunk before this; but, blessed be the God and rock of my salvation, here I am, and am perfectly satisfied and happy, having not the smallest desire to go one step backward. (Don C. Corbett, *Mary Fielding Smith,* pp. 36-37, 99-100.)

Even them will I bring to my holy mountain, and make them joyful in my house of prayer.... (Isa. 56:7.)

And it shall come to pass in that day, that the remnant...shall stay upon the Lord, the Holy One of Israel, in truth....For though thy people Israel be as the sand of the sea, yet a remnant of them shall return: the consumption decreed shall overflow with righteousness. (Isa. 10:20, 22.)

Mary may have been familiar with the words of Isaiah, but it is also likely that as she wrote, the Spirit brought to her mind these words, helping her to speak in the language of the fathers and to express the themes of the fathers. The Lord reveals many of the same truths to all generations, bringing together all of his words, both ancient and modern, for our good.

4. *Be familiar with the customs of, and manner of prophesying among, the Jews.* Because of the wickedness of the people, Isaiah and other prophets often used types and shadows to illustrate their point. Their messages were, in effect, hidden in parables, symbolism, and picturesque metaphors. This manner of prophesying was not unique to the prophet Isaiah, but was common among the prophets, including the Savior.

Since parables do not directly state the exact message, those who do not want the message are able to use the parable for some other means. Parables and metaphors can be used by those who so choose to camouflage the true meaning, or to divert the mind to some other topic. The Lord does not force upon the wicked what they already know and reject. The Savior spoke in parables because "they seeing see not; and hearing they hear not, neither do they understand." (Matt. 13:13.) But he "who hath ears to hear, let him hear." (Matt. 13:9.) When asked why he spoke in parables, the Savior quoted Isaiah 6:10:

And the disciples came, and said unto him, Why speakest thou unto them in parables? He answered and said unto them, Because it is given unto you to know the mysteries of the kingdom of heaven, but to them it is not given. For whosoever hath, to him shall be given, and he shall have more abundance: but whosoever hath not, from him shall be taken away even that he hath. Therefore speak I to them in parables: because they seeing see not; and hearing they hear not, neither do they understand. And in them is fulfilled the prophecy of Esaias, which saith, By hearing ye shall hear, and shall not understand; and seeing ye shall see, and shall not perceive: For this people's heart is waxed gross, and their ears are dull of hearing, and their eyes they have closed; lest at any time they should see with their eyes, and hear with their ears, and should understand with their heart, and should be converted, and I should heal them. (Matt. 13:10-15.)

Since the wickedness in Isaiah's day was similar to that in Jesus' day, the manner of prophesying was also similar. Elder James E. Talmage pointed out that some were

...too weak in faith and unprepared in heart to break the bonds of traditionalism and the prejudice engendered by sin, so as to accept and obey the saving word. Their inability to comprehend the requirements of the gospel would in righteous measure give Mercy some claim upon them, while had they rejected the truth with full understanding, stern Justice would surely demand their condemnation. (*Jesus the Christ*, pp. 296-97.)

When the Lord gave Isaiah his call, the instructions were, "Go, and tell this people, Hear ye indeed, but understand not; and see ye indeed, but perceive not." (Isa. 6:9.) This was a rather peculiar assignment. It causes those who do not understand "the manner of prophesying among the Jews" to wonder and question. The assignment was, "Make the heart of this people fat, and make their ears heavy, and shut their eyes; lest they see with their eyes, and hear with their ears, and understand with their heart, and convert, and be healed." (Isa. 6:10.) Isaiah did this by parables and other methods. Isaiah asked the Lord how long his assignment was to last, to which the Lord replied, "Until the cities be wasted without inhabitant, and the houses without man, and the land be utterly desolate." (Isa. 6:11.) In other words, if the people would not repent, the Lord did not want their hypocritical covenant-making and ritual observances. They would be destroyed and scattered, in spite of all the warnings Isaiah was to give them.

The true message of repentance, sanctification, and salvation was to the remnant that was to return in the last days. The Lord referred to this remnant as a tenth, or a tithing, of the people, that would be "a holy seed" in the last days: "But yet in it shall be a tenth, and it shall return, and shall be eaten: as a teil tree, and as an oak, whose substance is in them, when they cast their leaves: so the holy seed shall be the substance thereof." (Isa. 6:13.)

The state of disbelief and wickedness of the house of Israel at the time of Isaiah is described in Isaiah's first chapter. This ~apter can be considered a preface to the book of Isaiah, just as ~e first section of the Doctrine and Covenants was given as a pref-~e to the Doctrine and Covenants. Each serves as a voice of warning to all people. There are many similarities between the first chapter of Isaiah and the first section of the Doctrine and Covenants:

Isaiah	*Doctrine and Covenants*
Hear, O heavens, and give ear, O earth: for the Lord hath spoken, I have nourished and brought up children, and they have rebelled against me. (Isa. 1:2.)	Hearken, O ye people of my church, saith the voice of him who dwells on high, and whose eyes are upon all men; yea, verily I say: Hearken ye people from afar; and ye that are upon the islands of the sea, listen together. For verily the voice of the Lord is unto all men, and there is none to escape; and there is no eye that shall not see, neither ear that shall not hear, neither heart that shall not be penetrated. (D&C 1:1-2.)
But if ye refuse and rebel, ye shall be devoured with the sword: for the mouth of the Lord hath spoken it. (Isa. 1:20.)	And the rebellious shall be pierced with much sorrow; for their iniquities shall be spoken upon the housetops, and their secret acts shall be revealed. (D&C 1:3.)

The wicked state of the house of Israel, as explained in the first chapter of Isaiah, helps us further understand why the Lord would not accept their type of repentance, and why Isaiah's prophecies had to be hidden in parables so as to be heard, but not understood, by the wicked. Nearly half of the first chapter is a description of the gross wickedness of the people: "Ah sinful nation, a people laden with iniquity, a seed of evildoers, children that are corrupters: they have forsaken the Lord, they have provoked the Holy One of Israel unto anger, they are gone away backward." (Isa. 1:4.) Isaiah told them that they would not repent: "Why should ye be stricken any more? ye will revolt more and more."

(Isa. 1:5.) Likening them unto Sodom and Gomorrah, Isaiah mocked them: "Hear the word of the Lord, ye rulers of Sodom; give ear unto the law of our God, ye people of Gomorrah." (1:10.) According to some of the ancient writings of the rabbis recorded in the Talmud, and also according to the Ascension of Isaiah, this comparison caused no little stir among the leaders of the house of Israel. Both the Talmud and the Ascension indicate that the comparison to Sodom and Gomorrah was one of the reasons Manasseh sought Isaiah's life:

> And Belchira accused Isaiah and the prophets who were with him saying: "Isaiah and those who are with him prophesy against Jerusalem and against the cities of Judah . . . and Jerusalem also he hath called Sodom, and the princes of Judah and Jerusalem he hath declared to be the people of Gomorrah." And he brought many accusations against Isaiah and the prophets before Manasseh. (Asc. 3:6-10.)

Just as the Lord has stated that he does not want the unrepentant to partake of the sacrament, so also Isaiah instructed Israel that the Lord did not want the unrepentant to offer sacrifices: "To what purpose is the multitude of your sacrifices unto me? saith the Lord: I am full of the burnt offerings. . . . When ye come to appear before me, who hath required this at your hand, to tread my courts?" (Isa. 1:11-12.) After further chastisement and rejection of their mechanical worshipping, the Lord stated through Isaiah, "And when ye spread forth your hands, I will hide mine eyes from you: yea, when ye make many prayers, I will not hear: your hands are full of blood." (Isa. 1:15.) A cleansing of sins through the atonement was offered them even though the Lord knew they would reject such an offer:

> Wash you, make you clean; put away the evil of your doings from before mine eyes; cease to do evil; Learn to do well; seek judgment, relieve the oppressed, judge the fatherless, plead for the widow. Come now, and let us reason together, saith the Lord: though your sins be as scarlet, they shall be as white as snow; though they be red like crimson, they shall be as wool. (Isa. 1:16-18.)

The parallels and metaphors in the next few verses are not as hidden as those in many of Isaiah's prophecies:

> How is the faithful city become an harlot! it was full of judgment; righteousness lodged in it; but now murderers. Thy silver is become dross... Thy princes are rebellious and companions of thieves: every one loveth gifts, and followeth after rewards: they judge not the fatherless, neither doth the cause of the widow come unto them. (Isa. 1:21-23.)

A judgment of doom is pronounced upon them:

> And the destruction of the transgressors and of the sinners shall be together, and they that forsake the Lord shall be consumed. For they shall be ashamed of the oaks which ye have desired, and ye shall be confounded for the gardens that ye have chosen. For ye shall be as an oak whose leaf fadeth, and as a garden that hath no water. And the strong shall be as tow, and the maker of it as a spark, and they shall both burn together, and none shall quench them. (Isa. 1:28-31.)

The manner of prophesying among the Jews was that of speaking in strong words, "sharper than a two-edged sword" (D&C 6:2), yet speaking in parables and metaphors, since the customs of the people were wicked, and the people rejected the messages and covenants.

The purpose of the prophets and the Melchizedek Priesthood is to prepare the people to stand in the presence of God. Some seven centuries before Isaiah, Moses and the Melchizedek Priesthood were taken from the people because they complained; they did not want to stand in the presence of God. By the time of Isaiah, King Manasseh and others were saying that God cannot be seen because "no man could see God and live." (Talmud, Yebamoth 324.)

A lesser priesthood and a lesser law were given to the house of Israel because they did not want the higher law and covenant. In a similar way, Isaiah's prophecies were given in such a manner as to provide the lesser portion to those who did not want the greater portion.

An example of one of Isaiah's "hidden" prophecies was a sign given to King Ahaz when the house of Judah was having trouble with the two confederates, Syria and Ephraim. Isaiah told Ahaz to ask a sign of the Lord as a witness that King Ahaz should accept Isaiah's warning for Judah to trust in the Lord rather than fear his enemies. King Ahaz replied that he would not tempt the Lord by seeking a sign. But Isaiah gave him a sign from the Lord, that of the birth of the Savior:

> Behold, a virgin shall conceive, and bear a son, and shall call his name Immanuel. Butter and honey shall he eat, that he may know to refuse the evil, and choose the good. For before the child shall know to refuse the evil, and choose the good, the land that thou abhorrest shall be forsaken of both her kings. (Isa. 7:14-16.)

Isaiah was telling King Ahaz at least three things: first, that both of the kings Ahaz feared would not last; second, that a remnant would remain even down to the last day; and third, that the Savior himself was evidence, or a sign, that these things would happen, and Ahaz' only need was to fear the Savior, who would be born of a virgin. The power of the Savior's virgin birth is certainly sufficient to take care of all the problems Ahaz had.

A most profound parable was used by the Savior to tell the priests and teachers of Israel that they not only knew who he was, but that they would kill him because they knew. This "hidden" prophecy was an obvious parable sharper than a two-edged sword:

> Hear another parable: There was a certain householder, which planted a vineyard, and hedged it round about, and digged a winepress in it, and built a tower, and let it out to husbandmen, and went into a far country: And when the time of the fruit drew near, he sent his servants to the husbandmen, that they might receive the fruits of it. And the husbandmen took his servants, and beat one, and killed another, and stoned another. Again, he sent other servants more than the first: and they did unto them likewise. But last of all he sent unto them his son, saying, They will reverence my son. But when the husbandmen saw the son, they said among themselves, This is the heir; come, let us kill him, and let us seize on his inheritance. And they caught him, and cast him out of the vineyard, and slew him. When the lord therefore of the vineyard cometh, what will he do unto those husbandmen? (Matt. 21:33-40.)

Matthew recorded that when the priests and Pharisees heard these parables, they perceived that Jesus spoke of them, and sought to "lay hands on him." (Matt. 21:45-46.)

Not only did wicked rulers of the house of Israel reject Isaiah's words in his day, but the above parable is evidence that this rejection was a perpetual inheritance of the house of Israel. These inherited "chains of their fathers" largely determined the Jews' future as a nation and people.

Their rejection was also a great determining factor on what scripture these people accepted and what prophecies they rejected. Scriptures containing direct prophecies of Jesus Christ, and other important doctrine, were either eliminated from the Jewish canon, or avoided. Some examples are the Ascension of Isaiah and the Book of Esdras. The Ascension states that the wicked king Manasseh had Isaiah sawn asunder because of his prophecies of Jesus Christ. Such prophecies of the birth of the Savior, the Son of God, giving the name of Jesus' mother as Mary, and including other details of the Savior's life on earth, would naturally be unacceptable as canonized scripture to the hard-hearted scribes and Pharisees.

Thus, a major influence on Isaiah's manner of prophesying was that he spoke to a people who did not want his prophecies.

5. *Be engaged in continuous and conscientious study.* Isaiah introduces us to this fifth key with these words: "For precept must be upon precept, precept upon precept; line upon line, line upon line; here a little, and there a little." (Isa. 28:10.) There is no substitute for practice. This fifth key can become more effective the more one continuously applies the four previous keys. Conversely, the more one studies the book of Isaiah, the more he becomes skilled at using the previous keys.

Diligent and continuous study of the book of Isaiah produces the same results as study of the Book of Mormon or repeated attendance at the temple. Each additional reading provides increased light and knowledge.

One who diligently seeks to understand the words of Isaiah will also find that the more one reads the words of Isaiah, the greater the love he will gain for both the Savior and the prophet Isaiah.

Another great reward of seeking to understand Isaiah is that the one seeking gains a habit of inquiring often of the Lord. As this habit is developed, it becomes a polished gem. The Lord has promised great and marvelous wisdom not written in the scriptures to those who receive his word: "And when they shall have received this [the Book of Mormon], which is expedient that they should have first, to try their faith, and if it shall so be that they shall believe these things then shall the greater things be made manifest unto them." (3 Ne. 26:9-11.) By applying the proper keys, the scriptures become a springboard to mysteries of God not found in holy writ, but available to bless and enlighten those who seek.

A Final Rule

Joseph Smith gave a useful rule for understanding the scriptures: "What is the rule of interpretation? Just no interpretation at all. Understanding it precisely as it reads." (HC 5:261.) Changing or adding to what is written often introduces misinterpretation. This key is simple enough, but its application must be used with the other keys to understanding scripture. For example, the early Jewish interpretation of the suffering servant in Isaiah chapter 53 was that it referred to Israel instead of Christ's suffering. Chapter 53 should be "understood precisely as it reads," without any other interpretation. However, it takes a previous knowledge of the atonement of Jesus Christ to be able to understand it correctly.

Another example is an incident found in chapter 7 of Isaiah: "Then said the Lord unto Isaiah, Go forth now to meet Ahaz, thou, and Shearjashub thy son, at the end of the conduit of the upper pool in the highway of the fuller's field." (Isa. 7:3.) Some Latter-day Saint students of the Bible have explained that King Ahaz was out inspecting his water supply because of the Syrian-Ephraimite threat of war against Jerusalem, that he wanted to see if his water supply was sufficient. However, this is not what the text states. In fact, the early Rabbis writing in the Talmud, the official Jewish commentary, gave a different view. They said that King Ahaz was trying to hide from Isaiah at the fuller's field, the place for washing clothes. Some wrote that Ahaz even went so far as to drag a fuller's trough, or wash tub, over his head, so as to flee from Isaiah unrecognized.

It is natural for a scholar to want to change a verse if he cannot understand it. He wants to change the meaning to something he can understand. Therefore, scholars who do not know a gospel principle often attempt to change Isaiah's words, but they would not need to if they understood the gospel. For example, R. H. Charles, not understanding that judgments upon the wicked were to be associated with the first resurrection (*Mormon Doctrine,* pp. 402-3) wanted to omit the word *resurrection* from the following phrase: "...and there will be *a resurrection and* a judgment in their midst in those days." (Asc. 4:18, pp. 36-37; italics added.) Although Charles was a fine scholar, he apparently did not know that the first resurrection accompanies a judgment at the beginning in addition to that at the end of the Millennium. Scriptures should be used to interpret the world instead of using the world and its ideas to interpret the scriptures.

Since the prophecies of Isaiah are primarily to the Latter-day Saints, to prepare us for the Second Coming, the words of Isaiah are truly of great worth unto us today. His words tell us how to prepare for the persecution and affliction now at our doors. His remedies provide an escape from the apostasy prophesied for our day. The words of Isaiah are truly marvelous. They are profound, beautiful, powerful, and full of spirit.

It is easy to understand why the Savior commanded us to diligently study the prophecies of Isaiah. It becomes even more apparent as we continually study the book of Isaiah. Through continuous and conscientious study we come to feel with Nephi, "My soul delighteth in the words of Isaiah." (2 Ne. 25:5.) But most important, the more we study the book of Isaiah, the more we become like Christ. Isaiah's words are the words of Christ. They are true and faithful. His prophecies *shall* be fulfilled. We *will* participate in the fulfillment of his prophecies one way or another. Our salvation depends on what we do with Isaiah's prophecies.

5
Visions of the Latter Days

It is evident from the previous chapters that Isaiah saw many events and conditions of the present day, including:
1. The wickedness of our day, similar to that of Sodom and Gomorrah. (Isa. 3:9.)
2. The wicked living only for pleasure. (Isa. 21:4.)
3. The attitude, "Let us eat and drink for tomorrow we die." (Isa. 22:13.)
4. Living by bribes. (Isa. 2:11, 33:15.)
5. Corrupt and unwise political and religious leaders. (Isa. 3:12; 9:16.)
6. The proud and rich not caring for the poor. (Isa. 3:15.)
7. Immortality. (Isa. 3:16-24; 4:4.)
8. Men being killed in wars. (Isa. 3:25.)
9. Wicked priests and leaders. (Isa. 24:2-6.)
10. Secret satanic oaths and groups. (Isa. 28:15-18.)
11. Atheist movements. (Isa. 5:18-19.)
12. Calling good things evil and evil things good. (Isa. 5:20-21.)
13. So-called intellectuals. (Isa. 5:21.)
14. Alcoholism and drugs. (Isa. 5:22; 28: 1-3, 7.)
15. Bribes in government. (Isa. 5:23.)
16. Flagrant wickedness. (Isa. 32:6.)
17. In spite of wickedness, a remnant of Israel living the true covenant and serving the Lord. (Isa. 10:20-22; 25:9; 26:21; 28:5.)
18. A day when the Jews would come into the true covenant. (Isa. 11:12-13.)
19. A day when the Arabs would come into the true covenant. (Isa. 10:24-34; 11:14-16; 60.)

20.   Great missionary activity. (Isa. 18; 62:6-7, 10.)
21.   Work of salvation for the dead. (Isa. 24:21-22; 42:6-7; 61: 1.)
Several scenes from the last days were recorded by Isaiah.

Scene 1: Current Events

One of the most prominent depictions in the prophecies of
Isaiah is that of the sin of Sodom. Isaiah prophesied: "The shew
of their countenance doth witness against them; and they declare
their sin as Sodom, they hide it not." (Isa. 3:9.) President Spencer
W. Kimball stated that the sin of Sodom and Gomorrah is that of
homosexuality. (Spencer W. Kimball, *The Miracle of Forgiveness*,
p. 78.) One needs only to visit some of the large cities of the United
States to see that today we are living in a time when Isaiah's statement is true. The countenance of the homosexuals "doth witness
against them" and homosexuality is advertised openly. Another
fulfillment of such prophecy is that demonstrators lobby openly to
demand that homosexuality be legalized.

Isaiah's description in Isaiah 5:18-21 of a people who call evil
good and good evil is very descriptive of events in our days. The
attitudes and tax laws against marriage and large families are based
upon evil principles "considered to be good." The Apostle Paul
stated that long hair was a disgrace for men, but a crown of glory
for women. (1 Cor. 11:14-15.) Yet, a news release in the BYU
Daily Universe quoted a federal government representative calling
the BYU dress standards "damaging and demeaning." Another
sign of the times is the claim by some psychologists, and other
misled individuals, that premarital sex relations are "good."
Calling evil good and good evil is characteristic of an especially
wicked world.

Another event of the last days evidently known to Isaiah is the
prevalence of bribing. In February 1980, when FBI agents exposed
a number of U.S. congressmen who had accepted bribes, one particular case illustrated the fulfillment of Isaiah's prophecies. A
senator who was interviewed by the press claimed that he was not
guilty of accepting bribes. He stated that he was conducting an
investigation of his own to expose those doing the bribing. When
asked why he spent part of the bribe money, he responded that if
he just kept the money, the bribers might become suspicious, so he
spent some of it. But Isaiah said that one should not even hold

bribe money in the first place: "He that walketh righteously, ...that shaketh his hands from holding of bribes,...He shall dwell on high." (Isa. 33:15-16.)

There have been many incidents in these last days that fulfill Isaiah's prophecies of Americans and Latter-day Saints caring for refugees from the gentile nations. Since 1975, refugees have escaped from Communist seizures of such countries as Vietnam, Cambodia, Laos, Korea, and Thailand. Approximately forty thousand Vietnam refugees were in the Pulan Bidong, Malaysia, camp in February 1980. Concerning the conditions from where these refugees came, Isaiah explained: "For thy waste and thy desolate places, and the land of thy destruction, shall even now be too narrow by reason of the inhabitants, and they that swallowed thee up shall be far away." (Isa. 49:19.)

Refugees came to America by the scores as fast as conditions permitted and sponsoring families could be located. One radio announcement indicated that of those coming from Cambodia to the United States in 1980, eighty percent came to Utah. Many of these families lived with Latter-day Saint families that helped them get established, learn the language, obtain jobs, locate housing, join the Church, or whatever else was appropriate. It is marvelous how the Lord brings to pass these latter-day scenes metaphorically depicted by Isaiah:

> Thus saith the Lord God, Behold, I will lift up mine hand to the Gentiles, and set up my standard to the people: and they shall bring thy sons in their arms, and thy daughters shall be carried upon their shoulders. And kings shall be thy nursing fathers, and their queens thy nursing mothers: they shall bow down to thee with their face toward the earth, and lick up the dust of thy feet; and thou shalt know that I am the Lord: for they shall not be ashamed that wait for me.... But thus saith the Lord, Even the captives of the mighty shall be taken away, and the prey of the terrible shall be delivered: for I will contend with him that contendeth with thee, and I will save thy children. (Isa. 49:22-23, 25.)

Kiet arrived by airplane in Salt Lake City with his wife, Phuong, and one-month-old baby, Khang. They had only the clothes they were wearing and a few things in one small handbag. Their sponsor family drove them home to Spanish Fork, Utah, where they were to begin a new life. These were three of forty thousand people from the Bidong refugee camp in Malaysia. Kiet had been captured in February 1975, and had been a prisoner of war for eleven months when he escaped and hid in the jungle for two months. In April 1979 Kiet and Phuong fled from Vietnam with ten others in a twenty-one-foot boat they had built while hiding in the jungle. As this little boat passed a Communist security station, one Communist guard saw them. But the guard did not suspect that they were trying to escape, since they were in such a small boat. For five days without food or water, they rode the ocean waves and swells, crossing the Pacific waters to Malaysia. Isaiah's prophecy that those (the Communists) who "swallowed thee up shall be far away" was being fulfilled. (Isa. 49:19.) "The captives of the mighty" were "taken away, and the prey of the terrible" were "delivered." (Isa. 49:25.) We have become the kings and queens who Isaiah said "shall be thy nursing fathers and . . . thy nursing mothers." (Isa. 49:23.)

Now thousands of others like Kiet and his family have become our sons and daughters, fulfilling Isaiah's words:

> For, behold, the darkness shall cover the earth, and gross darkness the people: but the Lord shall arise upon thee, and his glory shall be seen upon thee. And the Gentiles shall come to thy light, and kings to the brightness of the rising. Lift up thine eyes round about, and see: all they gather themselves together, they come to thee: thy sons shall come from far, and thy daughters shall be nursed at thy side. (Isa. 60:2-4.)

All of these current events are ample evidence that Isaiah truly saw our day. However, according to Isaiah and present prophets, the worst of our day is yet to come. The oppression of everyone against his neighbor can be expected to get much worse. (Isa. 3:5; 9:19-21.) "No man shall spare his brother. And he shall snatch on the right hand, and be hungry; and he shall eat on the left hand, and they shall not be satisfied: they shall eat every man the flesh of his own arm." (Isa. 9:19-20.) He predicted times of destitution and want:

> When a man shall take hold of his brother of the house of his father, saying, Thou hast clothing, be thou our ruler, and let this ruin be under thy hand; in that day shall he swear, saying, I will not be an healer; for in my house is neither bread nor clothing: make me not a ruler of the people. (Isa. 3:6-7.)

The destructions and indignation will be so great that "their slain also shall be cast out, and their stink shall come up out of their carcases, and the mountains shall be melted with their blood." (Isa. 34:3.) A description in Isaiah chapter 34 of the day of the Lord's vengeance is very similar to various passages in the Doctrine and Covenants:

Isaiah 34	Doctrine and Covenants
Come near, ye nations, to hear; and hearken, ye people: let the earth hear, and all that is therein; the world, and all things that come forth of it. (Isa. 34:1.)	All nations shall hear it. (D&C 88:94.) Hearken, O ye people...there is no eye that shall not see, neither ear that shall not hear...(D&C 1:1-2.)
For the indignation of the Lord is upon all nations, and his fury upon all their armies: he hath utterly destroyed them, he hath delivered them to the slaughter. (Isa. 34:2.)	Mine indignation is soon to be poured out without measure upon all nations. (D&C 101:11.) ...and in his fury vex the nation; (D&C 101:89.) ...inhabitants...consumed away and utterly destroyed by the brightness of my coming. (D&C 5:19.)
Their slain also shall be cast out,... and the mountains shall be melted with their blood. (Isa. 34:3.)	...they shall behold blood, and fire, and vapors of smoke. (D&C 45:41.)
And all the host of heaven shall be dissolved, and the heavens shall be rolled together as a scroll: and all their host shall fall down, as the leaf falleth off from the vine, and as a falling fig from the fig tree. (Isa. 34:4.)	The curtain of heaven be unfolded, as a scroll is...after it is rolled up. (D&C 88:95.)
For my sword shall be bathed in heaven: behold, it shall come down upon Idumea, and upon the people of my curse, to judgment. (Isa. 34:5.)	...his sword is bathed in heaven, and it shall fall upon the inhabitants of the earth. (D&C 1:13.) ...shall come down in judgment upon Idumea, or the world. (D&C 1:36.)
The sword of the Lord is filled with blood, it is made fat with fatness, and with the blood of lambs and goats, with the fat of the kidneys of rams: for the Lord hath a sacrifice in Bozrah, and a great slaughter in the land of Idumea. (Isa. 34:6.)	...let fall the sword of mine indignation...(D&C 101:10.)

For it is the day of the Lord's vengeance, and the year of recompences for the controversy of Zion. (Isa. 34:8.)	For this was the day of vengeance... (D&C 133:51.) ...the day when the Lord shall come to recompense unto every man... (D&C 1:10.)

There are many marvelous parallels between the wording in the book of Isaiah and the Doctrine and Covenants. In addition, the more complete and extensive descriptions in the Doctrine and Covenants often explain the meaning of the phrases and metaphors used by Isaiah. For example, the "sword of the Lord" in 34:6 is his sword of indignation in Doctrine and Covenants 101:10; and the nations "utterly destroyed" in Isaiah 34:2, who are left at the Second Coming, are destroyed "by the brightness of my coming" in Doctrine and Covenants 5:19.

The wickedness of our day is so great that it is as though the restoration of all things in the last days includes the restoration of all the wickedness and more that the world has ever known.

Scene 2: Glorious Events

Although the worst is yet to come, there are also wonderful and glorious events yet to transpire. Of course, the most glorious of all is the coming of the Savior in his power and glory. This event is prophesied by Isaiah throughout his writings. Scenes of the Second Advent are as much a major theme of Isaiah as the messianic passages concerning the Savior's first coming. Some of the more prominent scriptures concerning the Second Coming are found in the following chapters: 2, 3, 9-14, 21-22, 24-28, 30, 34-35, 40, 49-51, 63-64, and 66. There are also elements of the Second Coming in other chapters. There are a great many different types of events and scenes described by Isaiah concerning the Second Coming. Many of the events are those of destruction and punishment, and many are of blessings and salvation.

These two types of events described by Isaiah remind one of the phrase used by Malachi in referring to the Savior's coming: "Behold, I will send you Elijah the prophet before the coming of the great and dreadful day of the Lord." (Mal. 4:5.) Many of the events are dreadful and many are glorious—dreadful for the wicked and glorious for the righteous.

All events of the Second Coming will be dreadful for the wicked, even those that are glorious for the righteous. The very glory of Christ's appearance is the glory that will burn up the wicked at His coming:

> Therefore shall the Lord, the Lord of hosts, send among his fat ones leanness; and under his glory he shall kindle a burning like the burning of a fire. And the light of Israel shall be for a fire, and his Holy One for a flame: and it shall burn and devour his thorns and his briers in one day; And shall consume the glory of his forest, and of his fruitful field, both soul and body: and they shall be as when a standardbearer fainteth. And the rest of the trees of his forest shall be few, that a child may write them. (Isa. 10:16-19.)

> For, behold, the Lord will come with fire, and with his chariots like a whirlwind, to render his anger with fury, and his rebuke with flames of fire. For by fire and by his sword will the Lord plead with all flesh: and the slain of the Lord shall be many. (Isa. 66:15-16.)

While it destroys all the wicked not destroyed by previous events, the glory of the Lord will serve as a blessing and glory for the righteous, a source of light by day and night to replace the sun and the moon.

Isaiah explained one of the greatest phenomena yet to take place:

> The sun shall be no more thy light by day; neither for brightness shall the moon give light unto thee: but the Lord shall be unto thee an everlasting light, and thy God thy glory. Thy sun shall no more go down; neither shall thy moon withdraw itself; for the Lord shall be thine everlasting light, and the days of thy mourning shall be ended. (Isa. 60:19-20.)

Many of the scenes Isaiah beheld of our day will help fulfill the prophecy made by Nephi that "in the days that the prophecies of Isaiah shall be fulfilled men shall know of a surety, at the times when they shall come to pass." (2 Ne. 25:7.)

Scene 3: Ephraim, Judah, and Arab Nations

Isaiah's prophecies shed light upon the Lord's purposes concerning the nations of the earth in the last days. Those who diligently seek to understand Isaiah's words shall not want for confidence in this day of confusion in the world. For example, prophecies concerning the Church, the Jews, and Arab nations are very applicable to our present day. These prophecies are even more meaningful in light of such events as Sadat of Egypt entering into a peace treaty with Israel, and Iran's Khomeini and militants holding fifty Americans hostage with threats of death and hatred toward America.

President Joseph Fielding Smith proclaimed that such events mark the hand of the Lord in fulfillment of prophecy. (*Doctrines of Salvation* 3:27, 33-34.) In chapter 60, Isaiah tells those of Zion, the chosen seed, to arise and shine, for "the Gentiles shall come to thy light." Speaking of the missionary work of the gathering, Isaiah states, "All they gather themselves together, they come to thee: thy sons shall come from far, and thy daughters shall be nursed at thy side." (Isa. 60:4.)

Isaiah further explains that after the forces of the Gentiles are gathered into Zion, Arab nations should next be gathered. The five Arab tribes and nations mentioned are (1) Midian, the son of Keturah (wife of Abraham after Sarah's death); (2) Ephah, one of the Midianite tribes; (3) Sheba, son of Jokshan, another son of Keturah; (4) Kedar, a son of Ishmael who was the son of Hagar, Sarah's handmaid; and (5) Nebaioth, another son and firstborn of Ishmael. Isaiah tells us that various Arab nations will come into the true covenant and help build up the kingdom in such a manner that: "thy gates shall be opened continually; they shall not be shut day or night, that men may bring unto thee the forces of the Gentiles and that their kings may be brought." (Isa. 60:11.) But those nations that do not accept the missionaries and the gospel can expect to be brought to their knees: "For the nation and kingdom that will not serve thee shall perish, yea, those nations shall be utterly wasted." (Isa. 60:12.)

Missionary work in many nations has been hindered by wars and other destructive forces. After limited success in Vietnam, the missionaries were suddenly taken out when communist forces took over in 1965. Fulfillment of the above prophecy from Isaiah's flood of light is occurring the world over.

One of the exciting passages in chapter 11 is somewhat of a travelogue through the annals of latter-day history. After the initial restoration by the Prophet Joseph Smith as an ensign set up to the Gentiles, the remnant is gathered in from various lands and the isles of the sea:

> And in that day there shall be a root of Jesse, which shall stand for an ensign of the people; to it shall the Gentiles seek: and his rest shall be glorious. And it shall come to pass in that day, that the Lord shall set his hand again the second time to recover the remnant of his people, which shall be left, from Assyria, and from Egypt, and from Pathros, and from Cush, and from Elam, and from Shinar, and from Hamath, and from the islands of the sea. (Isa. 11:10-11.)

Next follows the day of the Jews, when they begin to come to the ensign, gathered in from the four corners of the earth.

The Lord's Purposes Concerning the Nations

Isaiah's prophecies shed light upon the Lord's purposes concerning the nations of the earth in the last days.

1. *The restoration:* "And he shall set up an ensign for the nations, and shall assemble the outcasts of Israel, and gather together the dispersed of Judah from the four corners of the earth." (Isa. 11:12.)
2. *A certain unity; Jews and the Church:* "The envy also of Ephraim shall depart, and the adversaries of Judah shall be cut off: Ephraim shall not envy Judah, and Judah shall not vex Ephraim." (Isa. 11:13.)
3. *Arab nations to submit:* "But they shall fly upon the shoulders of the Philistines toward the west; they shall spoil them of the east . . . upon Edom and Moab; and the children of Ammon shall obey them." (Isa. 11:14.)

Who is Judah? The Jews. Who is Ephraim? Those of the birthright, the leaders of the kingdom, the Church. This harmony between Judah and Ephraim is something never before experienced, due to the early envy and jealousy inherited from Judah himself toward the chosen son of Joseph. News releases of the day confirm and fulfill this latter-day prophecy. Judah has given Ephraim a position on its famous Mount Olivet for a historical monument of peace, the Orson Hyde Memorial. The *Jerusalem Post* referred to President Spencer W. Kimball as a "prophet in the line of Abraham and Moses." (*Church News,*

Dec. 29, 1979, p. 5.) Judah has also publicly announced its confirmation and concurrence with Ephraim's stand on the so-called Equal Rights Amendment.

After an ensign is established and the gathering commenced, the Arabs will begin to submit to Ephraim and Judah as they come into the kingdom after some conflicts. Current events reveal the fact that Scene 3 (Ephraim, Judah, and Arab nations) from Isaiah's panoramic visions of the last days is presently on stage.

Scene 4: Pre-Millennial Events

The curtain is yet to be opened upon future scenes that will help make clear the penetrating prophecies of Isaiah as we behold their fulfillment. These marvelous events of the last days will include signs of the Second Coming, miracles to preserve the sanctified, and the powers of heaven that submit the enemies of the Saints to their power. In addition to the fire and glory of the Second Coming, other forces of vengeance will be dreadful for the wicked, but serve as blessings for the righteous. Isaiah warned: "Whosoever shall gather together against thee shall fall *for thy sake.*" (Isa. 54:15; italics added.) This same concept is expressed in the Doctrine and Covenants:

> I have sworn, and the decree hath gone forth by a former commandment which I have given unto you, that I would let fall the sword of mine indignation *in behalf of my people*; and even as I have said, it shall come to pass. (D&C 101:10; italics added.)

The extent to which destructions promised by Isaiah will occur in behalf of the Saints is further explained by the Lord in the Doctrine and Covenants:

> Mine indignation is soon to be poured out without measure upon all nations; and this will I do when the cup of their iniquity is full. And in that day all who are found upon the watch tower, or in other words, all mine Israel, shall be saved. (D&C 101:11-12.)

Calamities and destructions serve as a shield of protection for the righteous against the wicked. Isaiah explained that such works of the Lord will be to turn those who once were the enemies of the Saints to serve and obey them:

Then thou shalt see, and flow together, and thine heart shall fear, and be enlarged; because the abundance of the sea shall be converted unto thee, the forces of the Gentiles shall come unto thee. (Isa. 60:5.)

The sons also of them that afflicted thee shall come bending unto thee; and all they that despised thee shall bow themselves down at the soles of thy feet; and they shall call thee, The city of the Lord, The Zion of the Holy One of Israel. (Isa. 60:14.)

The historical waywardness of Egypt can be expected to change to true worship in the new and everlasting covenant:

And the Lord shall be known to Egypt, and the Egyptians shall know the Lord in that day, and shall do sacrifice and oblation; yea, they shall vow a vow unto the Lord, and perform it. And the Lord shall smite Egypt: he shall smite and heal it: and they shall return even to the Lord, and he shall be intreated of them, and shall heal them. (Isa. 19:21-22.)

Egypt's efforts at peace will be more complete and effective when they are based upon conversion to the gospel, along with Assyria and Israel:

In that day shall there be a highway out of Egypt to Assyria, and the Assyrian shall come into Egypt, and the Egyptian into Assyria, and the Egyptians shall serve with the Assyrians. In that day shall Israel be the third with Egypt and with Assyria, even a blessing in the midst of the land: Whom the Lord of hosts shall bless, saying, Blessed be Egypt my people, and Assyria the work of my hands, and Israel mine inheritance. (Isa. 19:23-25.)

Another future event prophesied by Isaiah entails the two missionary "sons" of Jerusalem who lie at the head of the streets when the Savior comes:

These two things [sons] are come unto thee; who shall be sorry for thee? desolation, and destruction, and the famine, and the sword: by whom shall I comfort thee? Thy sons have fainted, they lie at the head of all the streets, as a wild bull in a net: they are full of the fury of the Lord, the rebuke of thy God.

Therefore hear now this, thou afflicted, and drunken, but not with wine: Thus saith thy Lord the Lord, and thy God that pleadeth the cause of his people, Behold, I have taken out of thine hand the cup of trembling, even the dregs of the cup of my fury; thou shalt no more drink it again: But

> I will put it into the hand of them that afflict thee; which have said to thy soul, Bow down, that we may go over: and thou hast laid thy body as the ground, and as the street, to them that went over. (Isa. 51:19-23.)

Scene 5: The Millennium

Isaiah beautifully depicted numerous scenes of the Millennium. Some millennial events described by Isaiah are not found in other scriptures.

1. The earth shall be full of knowledge, as waters that cover the sea:

> But with righteousness shall he judge the poor, and reprove with equity for the meek of the earth; and he shall smite the earth with the rod of his mouth, and with the breath of his lips shall he slay the wicked. And righteousness shall be the girdle of his loins, and faithfulness the girdle of his reins. The wolf also shall dwell with the lamb, and the leopard shall lie down with the kid; and the calf and the young lion and the fatling together; and a little child shall lead them. And the cow and the bear shall feed; their young ones shall lie down together: and the lion shall eat straw like the ox. And the sucking child shall play on the hole of the asp, and the weaned child shall put his hand on the cockatrice' den. They shall not hurt nor destroy in all my holy mountain: for the earth shall be full of the knowledge of the Lord, as the waters cover the sea. (Isa. 11:4-9.)

2. The Lord will create a flaming fire by night and a tabernacle by day:

> And the Lord will create upon every dwelling place of mount Zion, and upon her assemblies, a cloud and smoke by day, and the shining of a flaming fire by night: for upon all the glory shall be a defence. And there shall be a tabernacle for a shadow in the daytime from the heat, and for a place of refuge, and for a covert from storm and from rain. (Isa. 4:5-6.)

3. There will be bountiful planting and harvests; the light of Christ, or "sunlight," will be sevenfold:

> Then shall he give the rain of thy seed, that thou shalt sow the ground withal; and bread of the increase of the earth, and it shall be fat and plenteous: in that day shall thy cattle feed in large pastures. The oxen likewise and the young asses that ear the ground shall eat clean provender, which hath been winnowed with the shovel and with the fan. And there shall be upon every high mountain, and upon every high hill, rivers and

streams of waters in the day of the great slaughter, when the towers fall. Moreover the light of the moon shall be as the light of the sun, and the light of the sun shall be sevenfold, as the light of seven days, in the day that the Lord bindeth up the breach of his people, and healeth the stroke of their wound. (Isa. 30:23-26.)

4. Rivers, fountains, and springs will be everywhere:

I will open rivers in high places, and fountains in the midst of the valleys: I will make the wilderness a pool of water, and the dry land springs of water. (Isa. 41:18.)

5. The Lord will be our sun and moon, a continual light, never to go down:

The sun shall be no more thy light by day; neither for brightness shall the moon give light unto thee: but the Lord shall be unto thee an everlasting light, and thy God thy glory. Thy sun shall no more go down; neither shall thy moon withdraw itself: for the Lord shall be thine everlasting light, and the days of thy mourning shall be ended. (Isa. 60:19-20.)

6. Children will live to be a hundred years old:

There shall be no more thence an infant of days, nor an old man that hath not filled his days: for the child shall die an hundred years old; but the sinner being an hundred years old shall be accursed. (Isa. 65:20.)

7. Men shall build houses and plant gardens:

And they shall build houses, and inhabit them; and they shall plant vineyards, and eat the fruit of them. (Isa. 65:21.)

One can more fully understand the prophecies of Isaiah and apply them to our time by asking, "What exists today that these verses could be depicting?" Elder Bruce R. McConkie explained that the greatness of the era of restoration is yet to be fulfilled: "All things are not to be revealed anew until the Lord comes. The greatness of the era of restoration is yet ahead. And as to Israel herself, her destiny is millennial." (*Ensign,* Oct. 1973, p. 81.)

We anxiously wait for the curtain to open on some final scenes prophesied for the Restoration, the Second Coming, and the ushering in of the Millennium.

The messages from the present latter-day prophets are the same as those of Isaiah, additional evidence that Isaiah truly saw our day. The words of Isaiah are pertinent for our world of confusion, our need for security and peace, and our preparation for the Second Coming. Isaiah's prophecies are of great worth unto us today. Our salvation depends on what we do with the messages of Isaiah and the living prophets. They have a message of grave importance for us.

6

Isaiah Saw Joseph Smith

President John Taylor penned a profound statement that reveals to the world the greatness of the position the Prophet Joseph Smith holds relative to all other prophets: "Joseph Smith, the Prophet and Seer of the Lord, has done more, save Jesus only, for the salvation of men in this world, than any other man that ever lived in it." (D&C 135:3.)

Since Isaiah is the Old Testament prophet of the Restoration, and Joseph Smith the latter-day prophet initiating the fulfillment of Isaiah's prophecies, would we not expect that Isaiah saw Joseph Smith and his great works in vision? Would we not expect that the events related to the Prophet Joseph Smith and the Restoration would be one of Isaiah's major themes? This is actually the case. There are quite a number of prophecies in the book of Isaiah related to Joseph Smith and the Restoration.

Joseph Smith and the Book of Mormon

The most prominent and well-known prophecy in Isaiah concerning Joseph Smith is the reference to the coming forth of the Book of Mormon found in chapter 29 of Isaiah and quoted in chapters 26 and 27 of 2 Nephi. These prophecies of Joseph Smith bringing forth the Book of Mormon are as detailed in description as any other of Isaiah's prophecies:

> And the vision of all is become unto you as the words of a book that is sealed, which men deliver to one that is learned, saying, Read this, I pray thee: and he saith, I cannot; for it is sealed: And the book is delivered to him that is not learned, saying, Read this, I pray thee: and he saith, I am not learned. (Isa. 29:11-12.)

Nephi declared:

> But behold, I prophesy unto you concerning the last days: concerning the days when the Lord God shall bring these things forth unto the children of men. After my seed and the seed of my brethren shall have dwindled in unbelief, and shall have been smitten by the Gentiles; yea, after the Lord God shall have camped against them round about, and shall have laid siege against them with a mount, and raised forts against them; and after they shall have been brought down low in the dust, even that they are not, yet the words of the righteous shall be written, and the prayers of the faithful shall be heard, and all those who have dwindled in unbelief shall not be forgotten. (2 Ne. 26:14-15.)

Although the phrasing in verse 15 appears to contain quotations from Isaiah 29, Nephi stated that he was speaking by the Spirit. (2 Ne. 25:4, 11.) Both prophets, being filled with the spirit of prophecy, could be expected to prophesy in similar terminology and phrases. This is consistent with the "language of the fathers." It is also possible that the language of the fathers used by one prophet may have been acquired from his studying the prophecies of previous prophets and brought to mind in his own prophecies through the spirit of prophecy.

Isaiah chapter 29 begins with a woe pronounced upon Jerusalem, referred to as Ariel, "the city where David dwelt." Isaiah stated in verses 1 and 2 that even though the people of Jerusalem offer sacrifices, Jerusalem would still be destroyed. In verse 2 we are told that "it" will be unto the Lord like Jerusalem, that is, destroyed. The description of the "it" that follows in the next several verses points our minds to the Nephites and Lamanites, if we are familiar with events in the Book of Mormon: "And I will camp against thee round about, and will lay siege against thee with a mount, and I will raise forts against thee." (Isa. 29:3.) Nephi explained how his nation would "speak . . . out of the ground, . . . low out of the dust, . . . their voice . . . as one that hath a familiar spirit" (2 Ne. 26:16), after they were destroyed. Isaiah spoke directly to the Nephites: "And thou shalt be brought down, and shalt speak out of the ground, and thy speech shall be low out of the dust, and thy voice shall be, as of one that hath a familiar spirit, out of the ground, and thy speech shall whisper out of the dust." (Isa. 29:4.) Both Isaiah and Nephi explained that their destruction would "be at an instant suddenly": "Moreover the multitude of thy strangers shall be like small dust, and the multitude of the terrible ones shall be as chaff that passeth away: yea, it shall be at an instant suddenly.'' (Isa. 29:5.)

This sudden destruction in Moroni's day, A.D. 421, is also described in the traditions and records of the Lamanites' descendants existing today. Thor Heyerdahl, in his magnificent record of various Lamanite descendants, *American Indians in the Pacific*, describes a sudden destruction in the Americas. This great extermination of one race by another is pinpointed in time as occurring in Moroni's time period, between A.D. 375 and 450. (Thor Heyerdahl, *American Indians in the Pacific*, p. 223.) After Nephi and Isaiah referred to the apostate conditions, they turned their attention to the coming forth of the Book of Mormon.

Nephi's account throughout chapter 26 includes more detail than Isaiah's prophecy. The exact source of this section of Nephi's prophecy is not known. Was he quoting from an earlier and more complete record of Isaiah, or giving the entire prophecy through the Spirit? In either case, the original source was the same, the Spirit of God.

Even though Isaiah's description of Martin Harris and Joseph Smith is more brief than that of Nephi, it is still detailed enough to identify with certainty the episode of Martin Harris's visit to Charles Anthon:

> And the vision of all is become unto you as the words of a book that is sealed, which men deliver to one that is learned, saying, Read this, I pray thee: and he saith, I cannot; for it is sealed: And the book is delivered to him that is not learned, saying, Read this, I pray thee: and he saith, I am not learned. (Isa. 29:11-12.)

From these descriptions, it is evident that Isaiah's visions of Joseph Smith included detailed events of the Restoration.

Personification; for an Ensign, and for the Gathering

Other allusions in Isaiah to Joseph Smith and his work are not as detailed as in Isaiah chapter 29. In fact, were it not for the Doctrine and Covenants, some prophecies might go unnoticed. For example, background information from the Doctrine and Covenants is needed to appreciate the prophecy in chapter 49 of Isaiah. There are four servants that may be identified in Isaiah 49:

Israel, the Savior, a prophet of the Restoration in the last days, and Isaiah himself as the Old Testament prophet of the Restoration. One can appreciate chapter 49 of Isaiah more fully when he realizes that prophecy is often of multiple fulfillment. Several quotations from the Doctrine and Covenants and one from Joseph Smith's *History of the Church* will help illuminate this chapter. The Lord declared: "Wherefore, I the Lord, knowing the calamity which should come upon the inhabitants of the earth, called upon my servant Joseph Smith, Jun., and spake unto him from heaven, and gave him commandments." (D&C 1:17.) The next verse alludes to the fact that the Lord also gave commandments to others through the Prophet Joseph. In other words, Joseph was the key or pivotal prophet.

Joseph Smith exclaimed: "...as the envy and wrath of man have been my common lot all the days of my life; and for what cause it seems mysterious, unless I was ordained from before the foundation of the world." (D&C 127:2.)

Isaiah wrote: "Listen, O isles, unto me; and hearken, ye people, from far; The Lord hath called me from the womb; from the bowels of my mother hath he made mention of my name." (Isaiah 49:1.) The metaphor or personification here could apply to all four "servants."

The Prophet Joseph stated: "I am like a huge, rough stone rolling down from a mountain; and the only polishing I get is when some corner gets rubbed off by coming in contact with something else. Striking with accelerated force against religious bigotry... licentious and corrupt men and women—all hell knocking off a corner here and a corner there. Thus I will become a smooth and polished shaft in the quiver of the Almighty." (HC 5:401.)

Now note Isaiah's words in verse 2: "And he hath made my mouth like a sharp sword; in the shadow of his hand hath he hid me, and made me a polished shaft; in his quiver hath he hid me." (Isaiah 49:2.) This personification could also apply to all four servants.

In verse 5 a servant is speaking who is to "bring Jacob again to him [the Savior]." And then this servant states (I am using a more accurate translation than that in the King James Version), "That Israel may be gathered to him and I may be glorious in the eyes of the Lord and my God shall be my strength." (Isa. 49:5.) Since this is referring to the gathering and a prophet-servant who is to bring about the gathering in the last days, one might ask, "Who is the prophet that initially provided the gathering of the last days?" On December 6, 1834, at Kirtland, the Prophet Joseph received a revelation containing the following statement:

> Therefore your life and the priesthood have remained, and must needs remain through you and your lineage until the restoration of all things spoken by the mouths of all the holy prophets since the world began. Therefore, blessed are ye if ye continue in my goodness, a light unto the Gentiles, and through this priesthood, a savior unto my people Israel. The Lord hath said it. Amen. (D&C 86:10-11.)

This revelation is similar to that received by Isaiah. According to one version of the Bible, Isaiah prophesied: "Is it a light thing that thou shouldest be my servant to raise up the tribes of Jacob, and to restore the preserved of Israel? I will also give thee for a light to the Gentiles, that thou mayest be my salvation unto the end of the earth." (Isa. 49:6.) The phrase common to the Doctrine and Covenants and the book of Isaiah is, "a light to the Gentiles, that thou mayest be my salvation unto the end of the earth."

From these two verses one may ask, "Who was the prophet that provided the gathering and who was the prophet that served as a light to the Gentiles and restored the preserved of Israel?" Naturally, all prophets of the last days serve in this calling, but it was initially the Prophet Joseph Smith.

When the angel Moroni appeared to Joseph Smith on September 21, 1823, telling him of the gold plates and the Urim and Thummim, he quoted the eleventh chapter of Isaiah, "saying that it was about to be fulfilled." (JS-H 1:40.) This was as if to say, "Joseph, the events found in this chapter not yet fulfilled are now going to be fulfilled starting with you."

Other references to Joseph Smith's day are found in Isaiah's prophecies. Doctrine and Covenants 113 reveals that the first part of chapter 11 of Isaiah, verses 1 through 5, are fulfilled in the first and second coming of the Savior. Verses 6 through 9 are obviously about the Millennium. Next comes a very interesting set of verses, which Isaiah introduced with one of his favorite phrases, "and in that day." As one reads "with feeling" through verses 10-13, he will see that Isaiah was talking about the last days. Note verse 10: "And in that day there shall be a root of Jesse, which shall stand for an ensign of the people; to it shall the Gentiles seek: and his rest shall be glorious." (Isa. 11:10.) Doctrine and Covenants 113 reveals that the "stem of Jesse" is Jesus; the "rod" is a servant in the hands of Christ who is partly a descendant of Jesse and of Ephraim, "or of the house of Joseph, on whom there is laid much power" (vs. 4).

If this servant is Joseph Smith, this passage in Isaiah 11 can be considered as being fulfilled. In addition, Joseph more fully fulfilled this prophecy and description than any other prophet. The same evidently applies to "the root of Jesse." Doctrine and Covenants 113 says that the root "is a descendant of Jesse as well as of Joseph, unto whom rightly belongs the priesthood, and the keys of the kingdom, for an ensign, and for the gathering of my people in the last days." (D&C 113:6.) The servant-prophet is one: (1) to whom rightly belongs the priesthood and (2) the keys of the kingdom, (3) who is for an ensign and (4) for the gathering in the last days. Of all servants in the last days, the Prophet Joseph Smith best fits these four characteristics.

Isaiah 11:10-13 contains similar information. In these verses the "root" (1) stands for an ensign of the people, (2) to whom the Gentiles shall seek, and (3) whose rest shall be glorious. Joseph Smith's rest was certainly glorious, sealing his testimony with his blood. Mother Lucy Mack Smith described an incident at the family viewing of her martyred sons:

> I sank back, crying to the Lord in the agony of my soul, "My God, my God, why hast thou forsaken this family!" A voice replied, "I have taken them to myself, that they might have rest." ... I seemed almost to hear them say, "Mother, weep not for us, we have overcome the world by love; ... ours is an eternal triumph." (Lucy Mack Smith, *History of Joseph Smith*, pp. 324-25.)

What servant of the Lord fulfilled the prophecy in Isaiah 11:11-12? There are two clues, one in verse 11: "The Lord shall set his hand again the second time to recover the remnant of his people"; and one in verse 12: "He shall set up an ensign for the nations, and shall assemble the outcasts of Israel, and gather together the dispersed of Judah from the four corners of the earth." First, the latter-day restoration was for the "second time to recover the remnant"; second, the ensign was "set up" through the Prophet Joseph to "assemble the outcasts of Israel." The fulfillment of these prophecies was initiated by Joseph Smith (Isa. 11:10-12), continued with the prophets since his day (Isa. 11:11-14), and are in final fulfillment in the events ushering in the Millennium (Isa. 11:14-16).

Events Initiated by Joseph: A Stone Rolling Forth

Through the restoration of the gospel and missionary work, Joseph Smith was the servant who provided for the gathering of Israel and the establishment of the ensign. What is the ensign? It is the gospel of Jesus Christ, the gospel covenant, and the Church. (Bruce R. McConkie, *Mormon Doctrine*, p. 228.)

Isaiah saw many other events initiated by Joseph Smith. In fact, the establishment of the Church in the tops of the Rocky Mountains, prophesied in Isaiah 2:2-3, was initiated by Joseph Smith. On August 6, 1842, the Prophet stated: "I prophesied that the Saints would continue to suffer much affliction and would be driven to the Rocky Mountains, ... making settlements and build cities and see the Saints become a mighty people in the midst of the Rocky Mountains." (HC 5:85.)

Other scenes of the restoration beheld by Isaiah and initiated by Joseph Smith relative to the ensign included missionary work and the establishment of the stakes of Zion (Isa. 11:12; 18; 33:20; 49:22-23; 54:2; 60:1-5); the desert blossoming as a rose (Isa. 41:18-20; 43:19-21; 53:1-6); and events leading up to the Millennium (Isa. 1:26-30; 2:3; 4:2-6; 18:4-7; 29; 33:4-8; 49:5-6; 50:10-11; 51:11; 52:6-15; 54:11-17; 55-62; 65:9).

Isaiah saw Joseph Smith's day. He bore witness of him and the glorious events of the Restoration.

7

Isaiah's Message to the Saints

Since Isaiah saw the problems of our day, can we not expect him to give us some great warnings concerning these things? Would we not expect him to tell us what to do about the situation we find ourselves in today? This is in fact the case. Isaiah's messages are very timely and urgently needed. His prophecies will come to pass. What happens to us depends on how we give heed to his messages. His warnings will be fulfilled with calamities upon the heads of all those who do not heed them. There are great and marvelous promises in store for those who do repent and hearken unto the words of Isaiah.

The Basic Message

As might be expected, Isaiah's paramount message is for us to come unto Christ in a more determined manner, more diligently: "Seek ye the Lord while he may be found, call ye upon him while he is near." (Isa. 55:6.)

Why Prepare?

Foremost among Isaiah's warnings is for us to prepare for the Second Coming: "Howl ye; for the day of the Lord is at hand; it shall come as a destruction from the Almighty. . . . Behold, the day of the Lord cometh, cruel both with wrath and fierce anger, to lay the land desolate: and he shall destroy the sinners thereof out of it." (Isa. 13:6, 9.)

Why is it so important to prepare for the Second Coming? Those who are prepared will abide the day. What does it mean to abide the day? There are two types of abiding. One is to abide the glory of the Savior's appearance so as to remain among the righteous. The second is to abide the perils and afflictions prophesied to come upon us prior to that day.

Isaiah promised those who were properly prepared, "Thine eyes shall see the king in his beauty: they shall behold the land that is very far off." (Isa. 33:17.) What will happen to those who are not prepared to abide the Second Coming?

> And I will punish the world for their evil, and the wicked for their iniquity; and I will cause the arrogancy of the proud to cease, and will lay low the haughtiness of the terrible. (Isa. 13:11.)

> For, behold, the Lord will come with fire, and with his chariots like a whirlwind, to render his anger with fury, and his rebuke with flames of fire. (Isa. 66:15.)

One of Isaiah's most urgent messages is to prepare for the great afflictions, sufferings, and purging that are to come to all, members and nonmembers, righteous and wicked. Isaiah tells us that this purging in the furnace of affliction is necessary to punish the wicked and to redeem and sanctify the righteous: "In all their affliction he was afflicted, and the angel of his presence saved them: in his love and in his pity he redeemed them; and he bare them, and carried them all the days of old." (Isa. 63:9.)

This is the same message Job and Joseph Smith received:

> My son, peace be unto thy soul; thine adversity and thine afflictions shall be but a small moment; And then, if thou endure it well, God shall exalt thee on high; thou shalt triumph over all thy foes. . . . Thou art not yet as Job; thy friends do not contend against thee, neither charge thee with transgression, as they did Job. (D&C 121:7-8, 10.)

The promised reward for endurance is exaltation, but Isaiah informs us that we must pass through the fire of affliction to gain that exaltation: "Behold, I have refined thee, but not with silver; I have chosen thee in the furnace of affliction." (Isa. 48:10.) However, Isaiah joins the rest of the prophets in instructing us that if we are purged and redeemed, we can pass through the purging fire in safety. When the Holy Ghost is with us in our afflictions, we do not feel them as we otherwise would. Isaiah promises: "When thou passest through the waters, I will be with thee; and through the rivers, they shall not overflow thee: when thou walkest through the fire, thou shalt not be burned; neither shall the flame kindle upon thee." (Isa. 43:2.)

We are living in perilous times, a day of vengeance. The angels of destruction have gone forth. Isaiah's voice of warning is echoed by modern prophets.

Elder Bruce R. McConkie declared:

> I stand before the church this day and raise the warning voice. . . . It is a voice calling upon the Lord's people to prepare for the troubles and desolations which are about to be poured out upon the world without measure.
> For the moment we live in a day of peace and prosperity but it shall not ever be thus. Great trials lie ahead. All of the sorrows and perils of the past are but a foretaste of what is yet to be. And we must prepare ourselves temporally and spiritually. (*Ensign*, May 1979, p. 92.)

Joseph Smith stated: "It is in vain for persons to fancy to themselves that they are heirs with those . . . who have offered their all in sacrifice . . . unless they, in like manner, offer unto him this same sacrifice." (*Lectures on Faith*, p. 58.)

President Joseph F. Smith stated:

> We are in perilous times, but I do not feel the pangs of that terror. It is not upon me. . . . I propose to live so that I shall be immune from the perils of the world, if it be possible for me to so live, by obedience to the commandments of God and to his laws revealed for my guidance. No matter what may come to me, if I am only in the line of my duty, if I am in fellowship with God, if I am worthy of the fellowship of my brethren, I can stand spotless before the world, without blemish, without transgression of the laws of God, what does it matter to me what may happen to me? I am always ready, if I am in this frame of understanding, mind, and conduct. It does not matter at all. Therefore, I borrow no trouble nor feel the pangs of fear. (*Improvement Era*, July 1917, p. 827.)

Even if a person is not ready to abide perils and afflictions by being "swallowed up in the joy of Christ " (Alma 31:38), such afflictions may be used to drive him closer to the Lord. Being thus driven, he may come to that state of preparation by being purged and redeemed through affliction. One of Isaiah's greatest promises is: "Thou wilt keep him in perfect peace, whose mind is stayed on thee: because he trusteth in thee. Trust ye in the Lord for ever: for in the Lord JEHOVAH is everlasting strength." (Isa. 26:3-4.)

How to Prepare

Isaiah gives us plenty to do if we are to prepare for that great day. There are several key words and phrases in Isaiah's prophecies that help us understand how to prepare. These include *sanctified, redeemed, contrite spirit, wisdom,* and *knowledge.*

Sanctified.

We have already seen that it is the sanctified who are fully prepared:

> Lift ye up a banner upon the high mountain, exalt the voice unto them, shake the hand, that they may go into the gates of the nobles. I have commanded my sanctified ones, I have also called my mighty ones for mine anger, even them that rejoice in my highness. (Isa. 13:2-3.)

Isaiah's words mark the path to sanctification. Isaiah promised that he whose mind is stayed upon the Lord shall be kept in perfect peace amidst perils of destruction. He also said that the sanctified will be spared and remain as pure vessels to receive the commandments of the Lord in the last days. These two concepts are explained in the Doctrine and Covenants: "Therefore, sanctify yourselves that your minds become single to God, and the days will come that you shall see him; for he will unveil his face unto you, and it shall be in his own time, and in his own way, and according to his own will." (D&C 88:68.) If we sanctify ourselves, our minds will be single to God, and if our minds are single to God, the days will come that we shall see him face to face. What greater preparation could we have for the Second Advent than to have previously seen the Savior face to face, especially as the "Second Comforter"? Should we really expect to have this type of an experience in this earth life? Joseph Smith proclaimed:

> When any man obtains this last Comforter, he will have the personage of Jesus Christ to attend him, or appear unto him from time to time, and even He will manifest the Father unto him, and they will take up their abode with him, and the visions of the heavens will be opened unto him, and the Lord will teach him face to face. (*Teachings*, p. 151.)

The Doctrine and Covenants helps us understand Isaiah's prophecies by telling us how we may sanctify ourselves:

> And I give unto you, who are the first laborers in this last kingdom, a commandment that you assemble yourselves together, and organize yourselves, and prepare yourselves, and sanctify yourselves; yea, purify your hearts, and cleanse your hands and your feet before me, that I may make you clean. (D&C 88:74.)

One becomes sanctified by obtaining a remission of sins through the cleansing power of the Holy Ghost. The sanctifier is the Holy Ghost. Elder Bruce R. McConkie states: "To be *sanctified* is to become clean, pure, and spotless; to be free from the blood and sins of the world; to become a new creature of the Holy Ghost, one whose body has been renewed by the rebirth of the Spirit." (*Mormon Doctrine*, p. 675.)

Redeemed.

Isaiah gives a joyful promise to those who are redeemed at the Second Coming:

> Therefore the redeemed of the Lord shall return, and come with singing unto Zion; and everlasting joy shall be upon their head: they shall obtain gladness and joy; and sorrow and mourning shall flee away. I, even I, am he that comforteth you: who art thou, that thou shouldest be afraid of a man that shall die, and of the son of man which shall be made as grass. (Isa. 51:11-12.)

How does one know when he is on the path to redemption? The answer to this question is among the last instructions given to us by the prophet Nephi in the Book of Mormon: "For the gate by which ye should enter is repentance and baptism by water; and then cometh a remission of your sins by fire and by the Holy Ghost." (2 Ne. 31:17.) One who is redeemed has received a remission of sins by "fire and by the Holy Ghost." How does one then know when he has received a remission of sins by fire and by the Holy Ghost? Nephi states: "Yea, then cometh the baptism of fire and of the Holy Ghost; and then can ye speak with the tongue of angels, and shout praises unto the Holy One of Israel." (2 Ne.

31:13.) What does it mean to "speak with the tongue of angels" and just what is "shouting praises"? Nephi tells us that speaking with the tongue of angels is speaking by the power of the Holy Ghost:

> Do ye not remember that I said unto you that after ye had received the Holy Ghost ye could speak with the tongue of angels? And now, how could ye speak with the tongue of angels save it were by the Holy Ghost? Angels speak by the power of the Holy Ghost; wherefore, they speak the words of Christ. Wherefore, I said unto you, feast upon the words of Christ; for behold, the words of Christ will tell you all things what ye should do. (2 Ne. 32:2-3.)

Thus, a person knows his struggles for redemption have borne the desired fruits when he is able to prohesy or "speak with the tongue of angels" by the Holy Ghost and feels to "shout praises unto the Holy One of Israel." (2 Ne. 31:13.) Alma refers to this experience as singing "the song of redeeming love." (Alma 5:26.) It is no wonder Isaiah prophesied:

> And in that day shall ye say, Praise the Lord, call upon his name, declare his doings among the people, make mention that his name is exalted. Sing unto the Lord; for he hath done excellent things: this is known in all the earth. Cry out and shout, thou inhabitant of Zion: for great is the Holy One of Israel in the midst of thee. (Isa. 12:4-6.)

Contrite Spirit.

Isaiah seemed to hear us ask, "But how do we go about obtaining a remission of sins?" For the next shining gem we find in the path to sanctification given by Isaiah is that of a contrite spirit. We obtain a remission of sins through a broken heart and contrite spirit: "For thus saith the high and lofty One that inhabiteth eternity, whose name is Holy; I dwell in the high and holy place, with him also that is of a contrite and humble spirit, to revive the spirit of the humble, and to revive the heart of the contrite ones." (Isa. 57:15.) Nephi tells us that if we do not have a broken heart and contrite spirit, the redeeming power of the Atonement is not efficacious in our behalf: "Behold, he offereth himself a sacrifice for sin, to answer the ends of the law, unto all those who have a broken heart and a contrite spirit; and unto none else can the ends of the law be answered." (2 Ne. 2:7.) To have a broken heart and a contrite spirit is to experience great remorse of sorrow for wrongdoing through the Spirit, as we submit ourselves unto the Lord. Thus, a broken heart and contrite spirit is actually a gift of the Spirit, as are all spiritual operations. It includes weeping spiritually over the suffering the Redeemer has endured for us. In seeking to repent, we may pray diligently unto the Lord, asking for a broken heart and contrite spirit.

In the book of Helaman we read:

> Nevertheless they did fast and pray oft, and did wax stronger and stronger in their humility, and firmer and firmer in the faith of Christ, unto the filling their souls with joy and consolation, yea, even to the purifying and the sanctification of their hearts, which sanctification cometh because of their yielding their hearts unto God. (Hel. 3:35.)

Some of the greatest and most important "mysteries of God" to be unfolded to us are the fruits of a broken heart and contrite spirit unto a remission of sins.

Experiencing this wonderful doctrine of repentance is necessary to fully appreciate the eternal implications of Isaiah's beautiful promise: "For thus saith the high and lofty One that inhabiteth eternity, whose name is Holy; I dwell in the high and holy place, with him also that is of a contrite and humble spirit, to revive the spirit of the humble, and to revive the heart of the contrite ones." (Isa. 57:15.) These transcending concepts cannot be explained by human tongue, only communicated by the Spirit to those who have experienced a broken heart and contrite spirit. The more we experience these divine ordinances of godliness, the more we understand Isaiah. Conversely, the more we study and understand Isaiah, the more we are brought to seeking and experiencing the exalting ordinances.

Wisdom and Knowledge.

Isaiah wrote: "And wisdom and knowledge shall be the stability of thy times, and strength of salvation: the fear of the Lord is his treasure." (Isa. 33:6.) This passage brings to mind Joseph Smith's statement that a man is saved no faster than he gains knowledge:

Add to your faith knowledge, etc. The principle of knowledge is the principle of salvation. This principle can be comprehended by the faithful and diligent; and every one that does not obtain knowledge sufficient to be saved will be condemned. The principle of salvation is given us through the knowledge of Jesus Christ. (*Teachings*, p. 297.)

The admonitions of the last several presidents of the Church to study the scriptures daily appear to be the same message that Isaiah gives for the stability of our times and the strength of salvation. If the stability Isaiah promises includes abiding the perils of the last days until the Second Coming, this is a gem of great worth.

What lack I yet?

Isaiah adds yet another dimension to redemption. One must retain a remission of sins from day to day by caring for the poor and needy: "Wash you, make you clean; put away the evil of your doings from before mine eyes; cease to do evil; Learn to do well; seek judgment, *relieve the oppressed, judge the fatherless, plead for the widow.*" (Isa. 1:16-17; italics added.)

The rich young ruler asked the Savior, "What lack I yet?" He felt that he had done all else the Savior had indicated for him to become redeemed. But the Savior told him: "If thou wilt be perfect, go and sell that thou hast, and give to the poor, and thou shalt have treasure in heaven: and come and follow me." (Matt. 19:21.) Caring for the poor is the one thing that the rich young man could not do. Therefore he could not retain a remission of sins.

Isaiah promises the glory of the Lord as a reward for those who care for the needy:

Is not this the fast that I have chosen? to loose the bands of wickedness, to undo the heavy burdens, and to let the oppressed go free, and that ye break every yoke? Is it not to deal thy bread to the hungry, and that thou bring the poor that are cast out to thy house? when thou seest the naked, that thou cover him; and that thou hide not thyself from thine own flesh?

Then shall thy light break forth as the morning, and thine health shall spring forth speedily: and thy righteousness shall go before thee; the glory of the Lord shall be thy rereward. (Isa. 58:6-8.)

The promises Isaiah describes are like a most delicious fruit satisfying and expanding the whole soul. There seems to be no end to them:

> And if thou draw out thy soul to the hungry, and satisfy the afflicted soul; then shall thy light rise in obscurity, and thy darkness be as the noonday: And the Lord shall guide thee continually, and satisfy thy soul in drought, and make fat thy bones: and thou shalt be like a watered garden, and like a spring of water, whose waters fail not. (Isa. 58:10-11.)

King Benjamin tells us that caring for the needy is for the sake of retaining a remission of sins from day to day:

> And now, . . . for the sake of retaining a remission of your sins from day to day, that ye may walk guiltless before God—I would that ye should impart of your substance to the poor, every man according to that which he hath, such as feeding the hungry, clothing the naked, visiting the sick and administering to their relief, both spiritually and temporally, according to their wants. (Mosiah 4:26.)

The importance of caring for the poor and needy is also stressed in the Doctrine and Covenants. Here the Lord declares that our redemption depends upon our imparting to the poor and needy: "Therefore, if any man shall take of the abundance which I have made, and impart not his portion, according to the law of my gospel, unto the poor and the needy, he shall, with the wicked, lift up his eyes in hell, being in torment." (D&C 104:18.)

Through these simple acts, we prepare ourselves to stand in the presence of God. Those who retain a remission of sins until the Second Coming are promised perfect peace. All their afflictions will be swallowed up in the joy of Christ. (Alma 31:38.) Isaiah promises: "And my people shall dwell in a peaceable habitation, and in sure dwellings, and in quiet resting places." (Isa. 32:18.)

A Final Message

The last chapter of the book of Isaiah appears to give a final, special warning to the latter-day remnant. We have found that there are many interesting parallels between the book of Isaiah and the Doctrine and Covenants. The last part of each of these two books have striking similarities in their "language of the fathers."

Message	Doctrine and Covenants 136	Isaiah 66
Fear not enemies, for all things are "in mine hand"; be "humble and contrite."	A *Fear not thine enemies, for they are in mine hands* and I will do my pleasure with them. My people must be tried in all things, that they may be prepared to receive the glory that I have for them, even the glory of Zion; and he that will not bear chastisement is not worthy of my kingdom. Let him that is ignorant learn B wisdom by *humbling himself* and calling upon the C Lord his God, *that his eyes may be opened that he may see,* and his ears opened that he may hear; *For my Spirit is sent forth into the* B *world to enlighten the humble and contrite,* and *to* D *the condemnation of the ungodly.* (D&C 136:30-33.)	Thus saith the Lord, The heaven is my throne, and the earth is my footstool: where is the house that ye build unto me? and where is the place of my rest? For *all* A *those things hath mine hand made, and all those things have been,* saith the Lord: B *but to this man will I look, even to him that is poor and of a contrite spirit, and trembleth at my word* . . . And *when ye see this, your* C *heart shall rejoice,* and your bones shall flourish like an herb: and *the hand of the* A *Lord shall be known toward his servants,* and *his indig-* D *nation toward his enemies.* (Isa. 66:1-2, 14.)
Your brethren hated you and cast you out.	*Thy brethren have rejected* E *you and your testimony, even the nation that has driven you out; And now* D *cometh the day of their calamity, even the days of sorrow, like a woman that is* F *taken in travail;* and their sorrow shall be great unless they speedily repent, yea, very speedily. For they killed the prophets, and them that were sent unto them; and they have shed innocent blood, which crieth from the ground against them. (D&C 136:34-36.)	Hear the word of the Lord, ye that tremble at his word; E *Your brethren that hated you, that cast you out for my name's sake,* said, Let the Lord be glorified: but he shall appear to your joy, D *and they shall be ashamed. A voice of noise from the city, a voice from the temple, a voice of the Lord that rendereth recompence* F *to his enemies. Before she travailed, she brought forth; before her pain came,* she was delivered of a man child. (Isa. 66:5-7.)
Why marvel at such things the Lord has brought forth?	G Therefore, *marvel not at these things, for ye are not yet pure;* ye can not yet bear my glory; *but ye shall* H *behold it if ye are faithful in*	G *Who hath heard such a thing? who hath seen such* H *things? Shall the earth be made to bring forth in one day? or shall a nation be*

keeping all my words that I have given you, from the days of Adam to Abraham, from Abraham to Moses, from Moses to Jesus and his apostles, and from Jesus and his apostles to Joseph Smith, whom I did call upon by mine angels, my ministering servants, and by mine own voice out of the I heavens, *to bring forth my work.* (D&C 136:37.)

*born at once?*for as soon as I Zion travailed, *she brought forth her children.* (Isa. 66:8.)

Praise the Lord and seek him, ye that mourn, and ye shall rejoice.

J *If thou art merry, praise the Lord with singing, with music, with dancing, and with a prayer of praise and* K *thanksgiving. If thou art sorrowful, call on the Lord thy God with supplication, that your souls may be joy-* L *ful. Fear not thine enemies, for they are in mine hands and I will do my pleasure with them.* (D&C 136:28-30.)

J *Rejoice ye with Jerusalem, and be glad with her, all ye that love her: rejoice for joy with her, all ye that mourn* K *for her:... that ye may milk out, and be delighted with the abundance of her glory...As one whom his mother comforteth, so will I comfort you; and ye shall be comforted in Jerusalem.* And when ye see this, your heart shall rejoice, and your bones shall flourish like an L herb: *and the hand of the Lord shall be known toward his servants, and his indignation toward his enemies.* (Isa. 66:10-11, 13-14.)

The final warning message.

M *Be diligent in keeping all my commandments, lest judgments come upon you, and your faith fail you, and your enemies triumph over you. So no more at present.* Amen and Amen. (D&C 136:42.)

M For, behold, *the Lord will come with fire, and with his chariots like a whirlwind, to render his anger with fury, and his rebuke with flames of fire. For by fire and by his sword will the Lord plead with all flesh: and the slain of the Lord shall be many...And they shall go forth, and look upon the carcases of the men that have transgressed against me: for their worm shall not die, neither shall their fire be quenched; and they shall be an abhorring unto all flesh.* (Isa. 66:15-16, 24.)

These marvelous promises by Isaiah instill within those who diligently seek, a burning desire to obtain and treasure up these gospel gems. They can do so by continuously studying them through the Spirit. Other great and glorious promises are given for those who heed the word of the Lord:

1. Perfect peace and protection.
2. Exceedingly great joy.
3. Afflictions and sorrows swallowed up in joy of the Lord.
4. Great faith to supplant fears.
5. Ruling over oppressors.
6. Prosperity, "increase of the earth."
7. Led by the way that they should go.
8. Kept within the covenant.
9. Becoming sanctified.
10. Seeing the Savior in his beauty.
11. Inheriting the earth as the celestial kingdom.
12. Becoming joint heirs with Christ.

One final, glorious promise is:

> He giveth power to the faint; and to them that have no might he increaseth strength. Even the youths shall faint and be weary, and the young men shall utterly fall: But they that wait upon the Lord shall renew their strength; they shall mount up with wings as eagles; they shall run, and not be weary; and they shall walk, and not faint. (Isa. 40:29-30.)

Appendix A
When They Shall Come to Pass

Isaiah's prophecies were written specifically to us today. The following brief outline is a list of the major concepts and events in each chapter of the book of Isaiah. Skimming over the precepts and events in the sixty-six chapters can help us appreciate the general messages and themes Isaiah has for us. This brief review may also help us appreciate the extent to which Isaiah's words and prophecies can be applied to us personally.

Chapter	Precepts and Events
1	The wicked state of Israel comes from conditions, customs, and traditions of the Jews (1-15); call to repentance (16-25); restoration and latter-day destruction (26-30).
2	The Lord's latter-day temple, restoration, and gathering (1-3); the Millennium (4); call to repentance (5-9); Second Coming and warning to the wicked (10-22).
3	Destruction of Judah and gross wickedness of the house of Israel in the latter days (1-26); warning to members as well as nonmembers (4-26).
4	Apostate conditions, yet happy state of latter-day remnant (1-4); latter-day purging and promises for the righteous (3-6); millennial conditions (5-6).
5	Comparison of the Lord's kingdom in Judah to a vineyard (1-7); lack of good works and gospel knowledge are a reason for captivity (8-13); apostate conditions then and now (8-17); warning (14-25); the restoration and gathering (26-30).
6	Manifestation of the Lord to Isaiah and a special calling to

Isaiah, symbolizing the Savior's premortal calling (1-12); the remnant and holy seed (13).

7   Historical events concurrent with Isaiah's day (1-12, 16-25); the name of Isaiah's son symbolic of the latter-day remnant (3); prophecy of the Messiah (14-15); widespread destruction, a parallel of latter-day destruction (18-25).

8   Two witnesses to Isaiah's recording of concurrent historical events (1-2); the name of Isaiah's second son symbolic of the destruction to apostate Israel and the Gentiles (3-10); call to trust in the Lord (11-22) instead of other nations (6-10) and other things (19-22).

9   Concurrent history, prophecies of the birth of the Messiah and his millennial and eternal reign (1-7); concurrent conflicts and destruction from the Lord, a parallel to the latter days (8-21).

10   Warnings against evils of the day to ancient and latter-day Israel (1-4); Assyria as God's punishing rod upon the wicked nations (5-11); destruction upon ancient Israel and Assyria symbolic of the last days (12-34) and the Second Coming (16-19); the righteous remnant in the latter days (20-23).

11   The prophecy of the Savior (1-5); the Millennium (6-9); the restoration and gathering (10-16), including Jews (12-13) and then Arabs (14-16).

12   A glorious song of praise to the Lord to be sung by those in the latter days and the Millennium.

13   Destruction of Babylon, a type of the Second Coming.

14   Latter-day and millennial gathering of Israel (1-3); Babylonian destruction and millennial conditions (4-32); destruction as a personification of Lucifer's being cast out of heaven (12-20); destruction prior to the Second Coming (21-31); latter-day restoration (32).

15   Concurrent history similar to latter-day weeping and destruction.

16   Prophecies of concurrent destruction (1-14); latter-day and messianic prophecy (4-5).

17   A prophecy of concurrent destruction (1-14) intermingled with latter-day and millennial conditions.

18   Prophecy of latter-day missionaries being sent from

America to scattered Israel (1-7); restoration and gathering (3-7).

19   Concurrent and modern purging of Egypt (1-17); conditions of Egypt in the latter days and the Millennium intermingled; Egypt, Israel, and Assyria to become one in the covenant (18-25).

20   Concurrent history and prophecy (1-6).

21   Concurrent destruction projected to the last days (1-7).

22   Destruction, history, and apostate conditions of Israel (1-25); Eliakim personifies the Redeemer and the Atonement (20-25).

23   Concurrent conditions and prophecies concerning Tyre in Assyria with chastisement for false pride (1-18); latter-day conditions (17-18).

24   Latter-day destruction (1, 6-12) and apostasy (2-12); call to repentance and destruction (13-19); events of the Second Coming (19-23).

25   Song of praise to the Lord by redeemed Zion at Second Coming (1-12); prophecy concerning the Redeemer (8).

26   Song of praise concerning the Second Coming and special keys for abiding the day (1-18); the resurrection (19); special message to the righteous (20-21).

27   Latter-day destruction (1, 7-11); restoration (2-6); gathering (12-13); millennial trumpet and conditions (13).

28   Chastisement and purging of latter-day Ephraim (1-4); a righteous remnant (5-6) among the apostates who are cut off from the Church (6-8) and the rest of the apostate world (7-8); only those strong in knowledge of the gospel will endure (9-13); secret oaths (15); the Savior (16); desolation at the Second Coming (17-29).

29   The coming forth of the Book of Mormon (1-16, 18); restoration at the time of apostasy (4-24).

30   Chastisement for false trusts of ancient Israel (1-14); Isaiah's prophecies recorded for the latter days (8); restoration of the remnant (15-22); the Millennium (23-26); destruction at the Second Coming (27-33).

31   Chastisements for false trusts (1-3); trust in the world (arm of flesh) versus trust in the Lord (2-6); latter-day destruction and fear of the strength of Zion (7-9).

32 The Savior's reign and millennial conditions (1-5); apostate conditions of the last days and destruction (6-14); restoration and blessings upon the righteous (15-20).

33 Chastisement upon evil-doers prior to the Second Coming (1); prayers of the righteous (2-5); special message for the latter-days (6); latter-day evils and destruction (7-14); marvelous blessings for the righteous in their refined state of living (15-19); the Millennium and the strength of the Church in the latter days (20-24).

34 Conditions of the latter days (1-10); the latter days and the Millennium (11-17).

35 The Millennium (1-2); the Second Coming and the Millennium (3-10).

36-39 Concurrent history concerning King Hezekiah's reign.

40 Comfort of Jerusalem (1-2) and events of Christ's first coming (3); the Second Coming (4-11); latter-day conditions—Lord reasoning with Israel (12-31).

41 The Lord continues to reason with stiff-necked Israel in ancient and latter days (1-29); conditions at the restoration and Second Coming (15-20) concerning the Savior (27-28).

42 The Savior as the great judge, lawgiver, and creator (1-5); the call and covenant of the latter-day righteous to be a light to the Gentiles and to bring those in spiritual darkness unto the Lord (6-9); the song of praise by the righteous in the latter days unto the Lord (10-25); the hand of the Lord upon all things and all people according to their work (13-25).

43 Jehovah as the creator, redeemer, and God of all nations (1-28); the latter-day gathering (9-10); the Savior's witness as the Lord and redeemer of Israel (11-17); a plea for God's children to remember the Lord in all things (18-28).

44 The house of Israel as the Lord's chosen, and their promise of a spiritual and refined latter-day state (1-4); Jehovah's call to Israel to accept and unite in him as their Lord and redeemer (5-8); special message for the latter days (8); plea to reason with and trust the Lord rather than the things of man for a solution to latter-day problems (9-22); a song of praise by the redeemed of the last days for their blessings from the Lord (23-28); King Cyrus to

shepherd the rebuilding of the temple in Jerusalem two centuries later (28).

45 Prophecy concerning a Babylonian king by the name of Cyrus to come some two hundred years after Isaiah's day (1-13); God's witness and warnings to ancient and modern Israel (5-25); gathering and salvation of Israel (14-25); the Savior (21-25).

46 False gods are nothing before the Lord (1-13); apostate conditions of ancient and modern Israel (1-13).

47 Gentile nations personified as the apostate world, ancient and modern (1-15); fate of modern Babylon in the last days (9-11); destructions of the last days (9-15); the Second Coming (14).

48 Call to repentance to the covenant people of Israel, ancient and modern (1-22); the redemptive process (9-10); special message to gathered and redeemed Israel (16-21).

49 God's servants: Israel, the Savior, a latter-day prophet, and perhaps Isaiah personified (1-12); the scattering, gathering, and salvation of Israel (1-12); song of praise by the latter-day remnant (13-17); latter-day gathering from other nations (18-26).

50 Apostate Israel, ancient and modern, and a call to repentance (1-4); the Redeemer (5-6); promises to those who trust in the Savior (7-11).

51 Call to seek the Lord, with promises for the latter-day righteous (1-11); more promises to the redeemed (12-16); call to repentance for Israel in the latter days, when the two prophet missionaries will lie at the head of the streets of Jerusalem (17-20); redemption after affliction (21-23).

52 Call to Israel, with promise of latter-day remnant by power of the priesthood (1-6); latter-day gathering of the remnant (7-15); the Redeemer (13-15).

53 A marvelous prophecy of the Redeemer and the atoning sacrifice.

54 Restoration, gathering, and strength of the latter-day Church (1-13); promises to the afflicted in the latter days (11-17).

55 Call of redemption and gathering (1-5); a special message to the latter-day remnant with promises (6-13); a millennial state (12-13).

56 Call to repentance and obedience with a promise for the latter-day remnant (1-7); gathering from the evil world (8-12).

57 Apostate conditions and pride of the world in the last days (1-8); their rewards (9-13); great promises to the contrite (13-15, 18-19); state of the wicked (16-17, 20-21).

58 Modern Israel called to repentance from complacency and false worship (1-5); the true fast defined and glorious blessings promised to those who observe it (6-12); a call for the latter-day remnant to return to the true Sabbath, with glorious promises (13-14).

59 The reason prayers are not answered, and latter-day apostate conditions (1-8); judgments upon latter-day wickedness (9-18); great promises for the gathered remnant (19-21).

60 Call for the latter-day Saints to be an ensign and missionaries (1-5); a great gathering from the Arabian nations to Israel, with blessings (6-17); gathering from the isles (9-11); nations destroyed that will not come to the covenant (12); millennial state (18-22).

61 The Savior's mission (1-3); latter-day gathering with blessings upon Israel (4-11).

62 Latter-day gathering (1-5); missionary work (6-7); manner of gathering (8-12).

63 The Second Coming (1-19); redeemed through own and Christ's afflictions (9); Jews (with the rest of Israel) accept Christ as their father over Abraham (16-19). (More details in Doctrine and Covenants 133.)

64 The Second Coming continued (1-12) (similar to chapter 63 and Doctrine and Covenants 133); latter-day repentance; Israel recognizes her waywardness (6-12).

65 Apostasy of latter-day Israel (1-7); a righteous remnant established, others destroyed (8-12); blessings for righteousness contrasted with punishment for wickedness (13-16); conditions during the Millennium (17-25).

66 A final message: Come to the Lord (1-5); comfort to those who trust in the Lord (6-14, 24); the Second Coming (15-16, 24); chastisements against waywardness (17, 24); the gathering (18-21); the Millennium (22-23).

We have great reason to rejoice in the flood of light and knowledge in store for us as we understand these prophecies. May we truly say with Nephi, "My soul delighteth in the words of Isaiah." (2 Ne. 25:5.)

Appendix B
The Ascension of Isaiah

Translation Revised by L. La Mar Adams

The English translation of the Ascension of Isaiah, by C. H. Charles, was compiled using three different manuscripts: Ethiopic, Greek, and Latin. Since there were a number of passages translated by Charles that tended to be confusing or were obvious mistranslations, I retranslated them using a "reverse translation." Since the original text is assumed to have been written in Hebrew, I first translated the English into the Hebrew and then retranslated it back out of the Hebrew into English, only this time in terms of the "language of the fathers." The comments in brackets are mine.

The earliest known manuscripts of the book of the Ascension of Isaiah date back to the same time period as the Old Testament manuscripts. Some of the manuscripts of the Ascension were in circulation at the time of the Apostolic Fathers. The Apostolic Fathers were leaders of the Church living during the time of the New Testament Apostles. Writers in the first and second centuries, such as Origen, Tertullian, Justin Martyr, and Jerome quoted from the Ascension. Some copies of the manuscript of the Ascension are dated in later centuries. For example, a Greek papyrus fragment was believed to have existed in the fifth or sixth century.

Several Church scholars and leaders throughout the ages have tended to accept the authenticity of the Ascension of Isaiah.

Chapter 1
1. And it came to pass in the twenty-sixth year of the reign of Hezekiah king of Judah that he called Manasseh his son. Now he was his only son.
2. And he called him into the presence of Isaiah the son of Amoz

the prophet, and into the presence of Josab the son of Isaiah, in order to deliver unto him the words of righteousness which the king himself beheld.

3. And of the eternal judgments and torments of Gehenna [place or realm of punishment], and of the prince of this world, and of his angels, and his authorities and his powers.

4. And the words of the faith of the Beloved which he himself had seen in the fifteenth year of his reign during his illness.

5. And he delivered unto him the written words which Samna the scribe had written, and also those which Isaiah, the son of Amoz, and, also to the prophets had given to him, that they might write and store up with him what he himself had seen in the king's house regarding the judgment of the angels, and the destruction of this world, and regarding the garments of the saints and their going forth, and regarding the transformation and the persecution and ascension of the Beloved.

6. In the twentieth year of the reign of Hezekiah, Isaiah had beheld the words of this prophecy and had delivered them to Josab his son. And whilst he [Hezekiah] gave commands, Josab the son of Isaiah standing by,

7. Isaiah said to Hezekiah the king, but not in the presence of Manasseh, only did he say unto him: 'As the Lord liveth, whose name has not been sent into this world, and as the Beloved of my Lord liveth, and the Spirit which speaketh in me liveth, all these commands and these words will be made of none effect by Manasseh thy son, and through the agency of his hands I shall depart mid the torture of my body.

8. And Satan will serve Manasseh, and execute all his desire, and he will become a follower of Satan rather than of me.

9. And many in Jerusalem and in Judea he will cause to abandon the true faith, and Satan will dwell in Manasseh, and by his hands I shall be sawn asunder.'

10. And when Hezekiah heard these words he wept very bitterly, and rent his garments, and placed earth upon his head, and fell on his face.

11. And Isaiah said unto him: 'The counsel of Satan against Manasseh is consummated: nought will avail thee.'

12. And on that day Hezekiah resolved in his heart to slay Manasseh his son.

13. And Isaiah said to Hezekiah: 'The Beloved hath made of none effect thy design, and the purpose of thy heart will not be accomplished, for with this calling have I been called and I shall inherit the heritage of the Beloved.'

Chapter 2

1. And it came to pass after that Hezekiah died and Manasseh became king, that he did not remember the commands of Hezekiah his father, but forgat them, and Satan abode in Manasseh and clung fast to him.
2. And Manasseh forsook the service of the God of his father, and he served Satan and his angels and his powers.
3. And he turned aside the house of his father, which had been before the face of Hezekiah, from the words of wisdom and from the service of God.
4. And Manasseh turned aside his heart to serve Satan, the angel of lawlessness, who is the ruler of this world, Satan, whose name is Gift of Worthlessness. And he delighted in Jerusalem because of Manasseh, and he made him strong in apostatizing Israel and in the lawlessness which was spread abroad in Jerusalem.
5. And witchcraft and magic increased, and divination and auguration, and fornication, and adultery, and the persecution of the righteous by Manasseh and Belchira, and Tobia the Canaanite, and John of Anathoth, and by Zadok the chief of the works.
6. And the rest of the acts, behold they are written in the book of the Kings of Judah and Israel.
7. And, when Isaiah, the son of Amoz, saw the lawlessness which was being perpetrated in Jerusalem and the worship of Satan and his wantonness, he withdrew from Jerusalem and settled in Bethlehem of Judah.
8. Where also there was much lawlessness, and withdrawing from Bethlehem he settled on a mountain in a desert place.
9. And Micaiah the prophet, and the aged Ananias, and Joel and Habakkuk, and his son Josab, and many of the faithful who believed in the ascension into heaven, withdrew and settled on the mountain.
10. They were all clothed with priesthood garments, for they were all prophets, and had nothing with them but were otherwise

script. And they all lamented with a great lamentation because of the going astray of Israel.

11. And these eat nothing save wild herbs which they gathered on the mountains, and having cooked them, they lived thereon together with Isaiah the prophet. And they spent two years on the mountains and hills.

12. And after this, whilst they were in the desert, there was a certain man in Samaria named Belchira, of the family of Zedekiah, the son of Chenaanah, a false prophet, whose dwelling was in Bethlehem. Now Zedekiah the son of Chenaanah who was the brother of his [Belchira's] father, and in the days of Ahab, king of Israel, had been the teacher of the 400 prophets of Baal, himself had smitten and reproved Micaiah the son of Amada, the prophet.

13. And he, Micaiah, had been reproved by Ahab and cast into prison. And he was with Zedekiah the false prophet: they were with Ahaziah the son of Ahab, the king, in Samaria.

14. And Elijah the prophet of Tebon of Gilead was reproving Ahaziah and Samaria, and prophesied regarding Ahaziah that he should die on his bed of sickness, and that Samaria should be delivered into the hand of Salmanassar because he had slain the prophets of God.

15. And when the false prophets, who were with Ahaziah the son of Ahab and their teacher Gamarias of Mount Ephraim, had heard,

16. Now he was a brother of Zedekiah, when they had heard, they persuaded Ahaziah the king of Gomorrha [Samaria] and slew Micaiah.

Chapter 3

1. And Belchira recognized and saw the place of Isaiah and the prophets who were with him; for he dwelt in the region of Bethlehem, and was an adherent of Manasseh. And he prophesied falsely in Jerusalem, and many belonging to Jerusalem were confederate with him, and he was a Samaritan.

2. And it came to pass when Salmanassar, king of Assyria, had come and captured Samaria and taken the nine and a half tribes captive, and led them away to the boundaries of the Medes and the rivers of Gozan,

3. This Belchira, whilst still a youth, had escaped and come to Jerusalem in the days of Hezekiah king of Judah, but he walked not in the ways of his father of Samaria; for he feared Hezekiah.
4. And he was found in the days of Hezekiah speaking words of lawlessness in Jerusalem.
5. And the servants of Hezekiah accused him, and he made his escape to the region of Bethlehem.
6. And Belchira accused Isaiah and the prophets who were with him saying: 'Isaiah and those who are with him prophesy against Jerusalem and against the cities of Judah that they shall be laid waste, and against the children of Judah and Benjamin also that they shall go into captivity, and also against thee, O lord the king, that thou shalt go bound with hooks and iron chains,'
7. But they prophesy falsely against Israel and Judah.
8. And Isaiah himself hath said: 'I see more than Moses the prophet.'
9. But Moses said: 'No man can see God and live'; and Isaiah hath said: 'I have seen God and behold I live.'
10. Know, therefore, O king, that he is lying. And Jerusalem also he hath called Sodom, and the princes of Judah and Jerusalem he hath declared to be the people of Gomorrah. And he brought many accusations against Isaiah and the prophets before Manasseh.
11. But Satan dwelt in the heart of Manasseh and in the heart of the princes of Judah and Benjamin and of the eunuchs and of the councillors of the king.
12. And the words of Belchira pleased him exceedingly, and he sent and seized Isaiah.
13. For Satan was in great wrath against Isaiah by reason of the vision, and because of exposure wherewith he had exposed Satan, and because through him the coming forth of the Beloved from the seventh heaven had been made known, and His transformation and His descent and the likeness into which He should be transformed in the likeness of man, and the persecution wherewith He should be persecuted, and the tortures wherewith the children of Israel should torture Him, and the coming of His twelve disciples, and the teaching, and that He

should before the Sabbath be crucified upon the tree, and should be crucified together with wicked men, and that He should be buried in the sepulchre,

14. And the twelve who were with Him should be offended because of Him: and the watch of those who watched the sepulchre,

15. And the descent of the angel of the Church, which is in the heavens, whom He will summon in the last days.

16. And that Gabriel, the angel of God, and Michael, the chief of the holy angels, on the third day will open the sepulchre.

17. And the Beloved sitting on their shoulders will come forth and send out His twelve disciples.

18. And they will teach all the nations and every tongue of the resurrection of the Beloved, and those who believe in His cross will be saved, and in His resurrection into the seventh heaven whence He came.

19. And that many who believe in Him will speak by the Holy Spirit.

20. And many signs and wonders will be wrought in those days.

21. And afterwards, on the eve of His coming His disciples will forsake the teachings of the Twelve Apostles, and their faith, and their love and their purity.

22. And there will be much contention on the eve of His descension and His coming.

23. And in those days many will love office, though devoid of wisdom.

24. And there will be many lawless elders, and shepherds dealing wrongly by their own sheep, and they will rave them owing to their not having holy shepherds.

25. And many will change the honour of the garments of the saints for the garments of the covetous. And there will be much respect of persons in those days and lovers of the honour of this world.

26. And there will be much slander and vainglory at the approach of the Lord's coming and the Holy Spirit will withdraw from many.

27. And there will not be in those days many prophets, nor those who speak trustworthy words, save one here and there in divers places, on account of the spirit of error and fornication

and of vainglory, and of covetousness, which shall be in those, who would be called servants of that One and in those who would otherwise receive that One [e.g., inactive members and apostates].

28. And there will be great hatred in the shepherds and elders towards each other.

29. For there will be great jealousy in the last days; for every one will say what is pleasing in his own eyes.

30. And they will make of none effect the prophecy of the prophets which were before me,

31. And these my visions also will they make of none effect, in order to speak after the impulse of their own heart.

Chapter 4

1. And now Hezekiah and Josab my son, these are the days of the completion of the world.

2. After it is consummated, Satan the great ruler, the king of this world, will descend, who hath ruled it since it came into being; yea, he will descend from his firmament in the likeness of a man, a lawless king, the slayer of his mother.

3. Who himself even his king will persecute the plant which the Twelve Apostles of the Beloved have planted. Of the Twelve one will be delivered into his hands.

4. This ruler in the form of that king will come and there will come with him all the powers of this world, and they will hearken unto him in all that he desires.

5. And at his word the sun will rise at night and he will make the moon to appear at the sixth hour [noon].

6. And all that he hath desired he will do in the world: he will do and speak like the Beloved and he will say: 'I am God and before me there has been none.'

7. And all the people in the world will believe in him.

8. And they will sacrifice to him and they will serve him saying: 'This is God and beside him there is no other.'

9. And the greater number of those who shall have been associated together in order to receive the Beloved, he will turn aside after him.

10. And there will be the power of his miracles in every city and region.

11. And he will set up his image before him in every city.
12. And he shall bear sway three years and seven months and twenty-seven days.
13. And many believers and saints having seen Him for whom they were hoping, who was crucified, Jesus the Lord Christ, after that I, Isaiah, had seen Him who was crucified and ascended and those also who were believers in Him, of these few in those days will be left as His servants, while they flee from desert to desert, awaiting the coming of the Beloved.
14. And after one thousand three hundred and thirty-two days the Lord will come with His angels and with the armies of the holy ones from the seventh heaven with the glory of the seventh heaven, and He will drag Satan into Gehenna [realm of punishment] and also his armies.
15. And He will give rest to the godly whom He shall find in the body in this world, and the sun will be ashamed, and to all who because of their faith in Him have execrated Satan and his rulers.
16. But the saints will come with the Lord with their garments, who are stored up on high in the seventh heaven, with the Lord they will come, whose spirits are clothed. They will descend and be present in the world, and He will endow those, who have been found in the body, together with the saints, in the garments of the saints, and the Lord will minister to those who have kept watch in this world.
17. And afterwards they will be transformed, in their garments in their body of this world, from above.
18. Then the voice of the Beloved will in wrath rebuke the things of heaven and the things of earth and the mountains and the hills and the cities and the desert and the forests and the angel of the sun and that of the moon, and all things wherein Satan manifested himself and acted openly in this world, and there will be a resurrection and a judgment in their midst in those days, and the Beloved will cause fire to go forth from Him, and it will consume all the godless, and they will be as though they had not been created.
19. And the rest of the words of the vision is written in the vision of Babylon.
20. And the rest of the vision regarding the Lord, behold, it is

written in the parables according to my words which I publicly prophesied which are written in the book.

21. And the descent of the Beloved into the Sheol [spirit prison] behold, it is written in the section, where the Lord says: 'Behold, my Son will understand.' And all these things, behold they are written in the Psalms in the parables of David, the son of Jesse, and in the Proverbs of Solomon his son, and in the words of Korah, and Ethan the Israelite, and in the words of Asaph, and in the rest of the Psalms also which the Holy Ghost inspired, in those which have not their name written, and in the words of my father Amos, and of Hosea the prophet, and of Micah and Joel and Nahum and Jonah and Obadiah and Habakkuk and Haggai and Zephaniah and Zechariah and Malachi, and in the words of Joseph the Just and in the words of Daniel. [Some of these prophets lived after Isaiah and therefore, if this text was originally authentic, their names either had to have been added by the abridger of this text, or Isaiah gave them by revelation, as Nephi in the Book of Mormon told about John the Revelator's writings].

Chapter 5

1. On account of these visions, therefore, Satan was wroth with Isaiah, and he dwelt in the heart of Manasseh and he sawed him in sunder with a wooden saw.
2. And when Isaiah was being sawn in sunder Belchira stood up, accusing him, and all the false prophets stood up, rejoicing and laughing at Isaiah.
3. And Belchira, with the aid of Satan, stood up before Isaiah, deriding him;
4. And Belchira said to Isaiah: Say: I have lied in all that I have spoken and likewise the ways of Manasseh are good and right.
5. And the ways also of Belchira and of his associates are good.
6. And this he said to him when he began to be sawn in sunder.
7. But Isaiah was absorbed in a vision of the Lord, and though his eyes were open, he saw them not.
8. And Belchira spake thus to Isaiah: Say what I say unto thee and I will turn their heart, and I will compel Manasseh and the princes of Judah and the people and all Jerusalem to honor thee.

9. And Isaiah answered and said: 'So far as I have utterance, I say to ye: Damned and accursed be thou and all thy powers and all thy house.

10. For thou canst not take from me aught save the flesh of my body.'

11. And they seized and sawed in sunder Isaiah, the son of Amoz, with a wooden saw.

12. And Manasseh and Belchira and the false prophets and the princes and the people and all stood looking on.

13. But to the prophets who were with him, Isaiah said, before he had been sawn in sunder: 'Go ye to the region of Tyre and Sidon; for unto me only hath God mingled the cup.'

14. And when Isaiah was being sawn in sunder, he neither cried aloud nor wept, but his lips spake with the Holy Spirit until he was sawn in twain.

15. This, Satan did to Isaiah through Belchira and Manasseh; for the adversary was very wroth against Isaiah from the days of Hezekiah, king of Judah, on account of the things which Isaiah had seen regarding the Beloved,

16. And on account of the destruction through the Lord, of the adversary, which Manasseh had seen while Hezekiah his father was still king. And he did according to the will of Satan.

The Vision Which Isaiah the Son of Amoz Saw

Chapter 6

1. In the twentieth year of the reign of Hezekiah, king of Judah, Isaiah, the son of Amoz, and Josab the son of Isaiah came from Galgala to Jerusalem to Hezekiah.

2. And having entered Isaiah sat down on the couch of the king, and they brought him another seat, but he would not sit thereon.

3. And all the princes of Israel were seated and the eunuchs and the councillors of the king. And there were there forty prophets and sons of the prophets: they had come from the villages and from the mountains and the plains when they had heard that Isaiah was coming from Galgala to Hezekiah.

4. And they had come to salute him and to hear his words.

5. And that he might place his hands upon them, and that they might prophesy and that he might hear their prophecy: and they were all before Isaiah.
6. And when Isaiah was speaking to Hezekiah the words of truth and faith, they all heard the voice of the Holy Spirit.
7. And the king summoned all the prophets and all the people who were found there, and they came. And Micaiah and the aged Ananias and Joel and Josab sat on his right hand and on the left.
8. And it came to pass when they had all heard the voice of the Holy Spirit, they all worshipped on their knees, and glorified the God of truth, the Most High who is in the upper world and who sits on High, the Holy One and who rests among His holy ones.
9. And they gave glory to Him who had thus bestowed it on a man.
10. And as he was speaking in the Holy Spirit, in the hearing of all, he became silent and his mind was exalted and he saw not the men that stood before him,
11. Though his eyes indeed were open. Moreover his lips were silent and the mind in his body was exalted.
12. But his breath was in him; for he was seeing a vision.
13. And the angel who was sent to make him see was not of this firmament, nor was he of the angels of glory of this world, but he had come from the seventh heaven.
14. And the people who stood near did not comprehend, but the circle of the prophets recognized, that the holy Isaiah had been exalted.
15. And the vision which the holy Isaiah saw was not from this world but from the world which is hidden from the flesh.
16. And after Isaiah had seen this vision, he told it to Hezekiah, and to Josab his son and to the other prophets who had come.
17. But the leaders and the eunuchs and the people did not hear, but only Samna the scribe, and Joachim, and Asaph the recorder; for these also were doers of righteousness, and the good pleasure of the Spirit was upon them. But the people had not heard; for Micaiah and Josab his son had caused them to go forth, when the knowledge of this world had been taken from him, and he became as one dead.

Chapter 7

1. And the vision which Isaiah saw, he told to Hezekiah and Josab his son and Micaiah and the rest of the prophets, and said:

2. At this moment, when I saw a glorious angel, not like unto the glory of the angels which I used always to see, but possessing such glory and position that I cannot describe.

3. And having taken me by my hand he raised me on high, and I said unto him: 'Who art thou, and what is thy name, and whither art thou raising me on high? For strength was given me to speak with him.'

4. And he said unto me: 'When I have raised thee on high through the various degrees and made thee see the vision, on account of which I have been sent, then thou wilt understand who I am: but my name thou dost not know.

5. Because thou wilt return into this thy body, but whither I am raising thee on high, thou wilt see; for for this purpose have I been sent.'

6. And I rejoiced because he spake courteously to me.

7. And he said unto me: 'Hast thou rejoiced because I have spoken courteously to thee?' And he said: 'Thou wilt see how one greater also than I am will speak courteously and peaceably with thee.'

8. And His Father also who is greater thou wilt see; for for this purpose have I been sent from the seventh heaven in order to explain all these things unto thee.'

9. And we ascended to the firmament, I and he, and there I saw the Adversary and his hosts, and there was great fighting therein and the angels of Satan were envying one another.

10. And as above so on the earth also; for the likeness of that which is in this firmament is here on the earth.

11. And I said unto the angel who was with me: 'What is this war and what is this envying?'

12. And he said unto me: 'So has it been since this world was made until now, and this war will continue till He whom thou shalt see will come and destroy him.'

13. And afterwards he caused me to ascend above the firmament, which is the first heaven.

14. And there I saw a throne in the midst, and on his right and on his left were angels.

15. And the angels on the left were not like unto the angels who stood on the right, but those who stood on the right had the greater glory, and they all praised with one voice, and there was a throne in the midst, and those who were on the left gave praise after them; but their voice was not such as the voice of those on the right, nor their praise like the praise of those.

16. And I asked the angel who conducted me, and I said unto him: 'To whom is this praise sent?'

17. And he said unto me: 'To the praise of Him who sitteth in the seventh heaven: to Him who rests in the holy world, and to His Beloved, whence I have been sent to thee. Thither is it sent.'

18. And again, he made me to ascend to the second heaven. Now the height of that heaven is the same as from the heaven to the earth and the firmament.

19. And I saw there, as in the first heaven, angels on the right and on the left, and a throne in the midst, and the praise of the angels in the second heaven; and he who sat on the throne in the second heaven was more glorious than all the rest.

20. And there was great glory in the second heaven, and the praise also was not like the praise of those who were in the first heaven.

21. And I fell on my face to worship him, but the angel who conducted me did not permit me, but said unto me: 'Worship neither throne nor angel which belongs to the six heavens, for for this cause I was sent to conduct thee, until I tell thee in the seventh heaven.

22. For above all the heavens and their angels has been placed thy throne and thy garments and thy crown, which thou shalt see.'

23. And I rejoiced with great joy, that those who love the Most High and His Beloved will afterwards ascend thither by the angel of the Holy Spirit.

24. And he raised me to the third heaven, and in like manner I saw those upon the right and upon the left, and there was a throne there in the midst; but the memorial of this world is there unheard of.

25. And I said to the angel who was with me; 'Nothing of the vanity of the world is here named.' For the glory of my appearance underwent transformation as I ascended to each heaven in turn.

26. And he answered me, and said unto me: 'Nothing is named on

account of its weakness, and nothing is hidden there of what is done.'

27. And I wished to learn how it is known, and he answered me saying: 'When I have raised thee to the seventh heaven whence I was sent, to that which is above these, then thou shalt know that there is nothing hidden from the thrones and from those who dwell in the heavens and from the angels there. And the praise wherewith they praised and the glory of him who sat on the throne was great, and the glory of the angels on the right hand and on the left was beyond that of the heaven which was below them.

28. And again he raised me to the fourth heaven, and the height from the third to the fourth heaven was greater than from the earth to the firmament.

29. And there again I saw those who were on the right hand and those who were on the left, and him who sat on the throne was in the midst, and there also they were praising.

30. And the praise and glory of the angels on the right was greater than that of those on the left.

31. And again the glory of him who sat on the throne was greater than that of the angels on the right, and their glory was beyond that of those who were below.

32. And he raised me to the fifth heaven.

33. And again I saw those upon the right hand and on the left, and him who sat on the throne possessing greater glory than those of the fourth heaven.

34. And the glory of those on the right hand was greater than that of those on the left from the third to the fourth.

35. And the glory of him who was on the throne was greater than that of the angels on the right hand.

36. And their praise was more glorious than that of the fourth heaven.

37. And I praised Him, who is not named, even the Only Begotten who dwelleth in the heavens, whose name is not known to any flesh, who has bestowed such glory on the several heavens, and who makes great the glory of the angels, and more excellent the glory of him who sitteth on the throne.

Chapter 8

1. And again he raised me into the firmament of the sixth heaven, and I saw such glory as I had not seen in the five heavens.
2. For I saw angels possessing great glory.
3. And the praise there was holy and wonderful.
4. And I said to the angel who conducted me: 'What is this which I see, my lord?'
5. And he said: 'I am not thy lord, but thy fellow servant.'
6. And again I asked him, and I said unto him: 'Why are there not angelic fellow servants on the left?'
7. And he said: 'From the sixth heaven there are no longer angels on the left, nor a throne set in the midst, but they are directed by the power of the seventh heaven, where dwelleth He that is not named, even the Elect One, whose name has not been made known, and none of the heavens can learn His name.
8. For it is He alone to whose voice all the heavens and thrones give answer. I have therefore been empowered and sent to raise thee here that thou mayest see this glory,
9. And that thou mayest see the Lord of all those heavens and thrones,
10. Undergoing successive transformation until He resembles your form and likeness.
11. I indeed say unto thee, Isaiah, no man about to return into a body of the world has seen what thou seest or perceived what thou hast perceived and what thou wilt see.
12. For it has been permitted to thee in the lot of the Lord to come hither. And from thence comes the power of the sixth heaven and of the firmament.'
13. And I magnified my Lord with praise, in that through His lot I should come hither.
14. And he said: 'Hear, furthermore, therefore, this also from thy fellow servant: when in the body by the will of God thou hast ascended hither, then thou wilt receive the garment which thou seest that are like the designated garments of others, laid up which thou seest,
15. And then thou wilt become equal to the angels of the sixth heaven,' and there were no angels on the left, nor a throne in

the midst, but all had one appearance and their power of praise was equal.

17. And power was given to me also, and I also praised along with them and that angel also, and our praise was like theirs.

18. And there they all named the primal Father and His Beloved, the Christ, and the Holy Spirit, all with one voice.

19. And their voice was not like the voice of the angels in the five heavens,

20. Nor like their discourse but the voice was different there, and there was much light there.

21. And then, when I was in the sixth heaven I thought the light which I had seen in the five heavens to be but darkness.

22. And I rejoiced and praised Him who hath bestowed such light on those who wait for His promise.

23. And I besought the angel who conducted me that I should not henceforth return to the carnal world.

24. I say indeed unto you, Hezekiah and Josab my son and Micaiah, that there is much darkness here.

25. And the angel who conducted me comprehended what I thought and said: 'If in this light thou dost rejoice, how much more wilt thou rejoice when in the seventh heaven thou seest the light where the Heavenly Father and His only begotten Son are, from whence I have been sent, who is to be called ''Son'' in this world. But not yet manifested, He shall be in the corruptible world.

26. And the garments, and the thrones, and the crowns which are laid up for the righteous for those who trust in that Lord who will descend in your form. For the light which is there is great and wonderful.

27. And as concerning thy not returning into the body, thy days for coming here are not yet fulfilled.'

28. And when I heard this, I was troubled, and he said: 'Do not be troubled.'

Chapter 9

1. And he took me into the firmament of the seventh heaven, and moreover I heard a voice saying: 'How far will he ascend that dwelleth in the flesh?' And I feared and trembled.

2. And when I trembled, behold, I heard from hence another

voice sent forth, saying: 'It is permitted to the holy Isaiah to ascend hither; for here is his garment.'

3. And I asked the angel who was with me and said: 'Who is he who forbade me, and who is he who sanctioned me to ascend?'
4. And he said unto me: 'He who forbade thee, this is he who is over the praise-giving of the sixth heaven.
5. And He who sanctioned thee, this is thy Lord God, the Lord Christ, who will be called "Jesus" in the world, but His name thou canst not hear till thou hast ascended out of thy body.'
6. And he raised me up into the seventh heaven, and I saw there a wonderful light and angels innumerable.
7. And there I saw all the righteous from the time of Adam.
8. And there I saw the holy Abel and all the righteous.
9. And there I saw Enoch and all who were with him, stript of the garment of flesh, and I saw them in their garments of the upper world, and they were like angels, standing there in great glory.
10. But they sat not on their thrones, nor were their crowns of glory on them.
11. And I asked the angel who was with me: 'How is it that they have received the garments, but have not the thrones and the crowns?'
12. And he said unto me: 'Crowns and thrones of glory they do not receive, till the Beloved will descend in the form in which you will see Him descend into the world in the last days, the Lord, who will be called Christ.
13. Nevertheless they see and know whose will be thrones and crowns when He has descended and been made in your form, and they will think that He is flesh and is a man.
14. And the god of that world will stretch forth his hand against the Son, and they will crucify Him on a tree, and will slay Him, not knowing who He is.
15. And thus His descent, as you will see, will be hidden even from the heavens, so that it will not be known who He is.
16. And when He hath plundered the angel of death, He will arise on the third day, and he will remain in the world.
17. And then many of the righteous will ascend with Him, whose spirits receive their garments when the Lord Christ ascend and they ascend with Him.

18. Then indeed they will receive their garments and thrones and crowns, when He has ascended into the seventh heaven.'

19. And I said unto him that which I had asked him in the third heaven.

20. 'Show me how everything which is done in that world is here made known.'

21. And whilst I was still speaking with him, behold one of the angels who stood nigh, more glorious than the glory of that angel who had raised me up from the world,

22. Showed me a book, but not as a book of this world, and he opened it, and the book was written, but not as a book of this world. And he gave it to me and I read it, and lo! the deeds of the children of Israel were written therein, and the deeds of those whom I know, my son Josab.

23. And I said: 'In truth, there is nothing hidden in the seventh heaven, which is done in this world.'

24. And I saw there many garments laid up, and many thrones and many crowns.

25. And I said to the angel: 'Whose are these garments and thrones and crowns?'

26. And he said unto me: 'These garments many from that world will receive, believing in the words of that One, who shall be named as I told thee, and they will observe those things, and believe in them, and believe in His cross: for them are these laid up.'

27. And I saw a certain One standing, whose glory surpassed that of all, and His glory was great and wonderful.

28. And after I had seen Him, all the righteous whom I had seen and also the angels whom I had seen came to Him. And Adam and Abel and Seth and all the righteous first drew near and worshipped Him, and they all praised Him with one voice, and I myself also gave praise with them, and my giving of praise was as theirs.

29. And then all the angels drew nigh and worshipped and gave praise.

30. And I was again transformed and became like an angel.

31. And thereupon the angel who conducted me said to me: 'Worship this One,' and I worshipped and praised.

32. And the angel said unto me: 'This is the Lord of all the praise-givings which thou hast seen.'

33. And whilst he was still speaking, I saw another Glorious One who was like Him, and the righteous drew nigh and worshipped and praised, and I praised together with them. But my glory was transformed into accordance with their form.
34. And thereupon the angels drew near and worshipped Him.
35. And I saw the Lord and the second angel, and they were standing.
36. And the second whom I saw was on the left of my Lord. And I asked: 'Who is this?' and he said unto me: 'Worship Him, for He is the angel of the Holy Spirit, who speaketh in thee and the rest of the righteous.'
37. And I saw the great glory, the eyes of my spirit being open, and I could thereupon see, and also could the angel who was with me, and all the angels whom I had seen worshipping my Lord.
38. And I saw the righteous beholding with great power the glory of that One.
39. And my Lord drew nigh to me and the angel of the Spirit, and He said: 'See how it is given to thee to see God, and on thy account, power is given to the angel who is with thee.'
40. And I saw how my Lord and the angel of the Spirit worshipped, and they both together praised God.
41. And thereupon all the righteous drew near and worshipped.
42. And the angels drew near and worshipped, and all the angels praised.

Chapter 10

1. And thereupon I heard the voices and the giving of praise, which I had heard in each of the six heavens, ascending and being heard there.
2. And all were being sent up to that Glorious One whose glory I beheld.
3. And I myself was hearing and beholding the praise which was given to Him.
4. And the Lord and the angel of the Spirit were beholding all and hearing all.
5. And all the praises which are sent up from the six heavens are not only heard, but seen.
6. And I heard the angel who conducted me, and he said: 'This is the Most High of the high ones, dwelling in the holy world, and resting in His holy ones, who will be called by the Holy

Spirit through the lips of the righteous the Father of the Lord.'

7. And I heard the voice of the Most High, the Father of my Lord, saying to my Lord Christ who will be called Jesus:

8. 'Go forth and descend through all the heavens, and thou wilt descend to the firmament and that world: to the angel in Sheol [spirit prison] thou wilt descend, but to the Realm of Punishment thou wilt not go.

9. And thou wilt become like unto the likeness of all who are in the five heavens.

10. And thou wilt be careful to become like the form of the angels of the firmament and the angels also who are in Sheol.

11. And none of the angels of that world shall know that Thou art Lord with Me of the seven heavens and of their angels.

12. And they shall not know that Thou art with Me, till with a loud voice I have called to the heavens, and their angels and their lights, even unto the sixth heaven, in order that you mayst judge and destroy the princes and angels and gods of that world, and the world that is dominated by them.

13. For they have denied Me and said: "We alone are, and there is none beside us."

14. And afterwards when thou hast died and risen, Thou wilt ascend to Thy place. And Thou wilt not be transformed in each heaven, but in glory wilt Thou ascend and sit on My right hand.

15. And thereupon the princes and powers of the world will worship Thee.'

16. These commands I heard the Great Glory giving to my Lord.

17. And thus I saw my Lord go forth from the seventh heaven into the sixth heaven.

18. And the angel who conducted me from the world was with me and said unto me: 'Understand, Isaiah, and behold the transformation and descent of the Lord.'

19. And I beheld that when the angels in the sixth heaven saw Him, they praised and lauded Him; for He had not been transformed after the shape of the angels there, and I also praised with them.

20. And I saw when He descended into the fifth heaven, that in the fifth heaven He made Himself like unto the form of the angels

there, and they did not praise Him nor worship Him; for His form was like unto theirs.

21. And then He descended into the fourth heaven, and made Himself like unto the form of the angels there.

22. And when they saw Him, they did not praise or laud Him; for His form was like unto their form.

23. And again I beheld that when He descended into the third heaven, that He made Himself like unto the form of the angels in the third heaven.

24. And those who kept the gate of the third heaven demanded the password, and the Lord gave it to them in order that He should not be recognized. And when they saw Him, they did not praise or laud Him; for His form was like unto their form.

25. And again I saw when He descended into the second heaven, and again He gave the password there; those who kept the gate proceeded to demand and the Lord to give.

26. And I saw when He made Himself like unto the form of the angels in the second heaven, and they saw Him and they did not praise Him; for His form was like unto their form.

27. And again I saw when He descended into the first heaven, and there also He gave the password to those who kept the gate, and He made Himself like unto the form of the angels who were on the left of that throne, and they neither praised nor lauded Him; for His form was like unto their form.

28. But as for me, no one asked me on account of the angel who conducted me.

29. And again He descended into the firmament where dwelleth the ruler of this world, and He gave the password to those on the left, and His form was like theirs, and they did not praise Him there; but they were envying one another and fighting; for here there is a power of evil and envying about trifles.

30. And I saw when He descended and made Himself like unto the angels of the firmament, and He was like one of them.

31. And He gave no password; for there was plundering and doing violence to one another.

Chapter 11

1. After this I beheld that the angel who spoke with me, who

conducted me, said unto me: 'Understand, Isaiah son of Amoz; for for this purpose have I been sent from God.'

2. And I indeed saw a woman of the family of David the prophet, named Mary, a Virgin, and she was espoused to a man named Joseph, a carpenter, and he also was of the seed and family of the righteous David of Bethlehem Judah.

3. And he came into his lot. And when she was espoused, she was found with child, and Joseph the carpenter was desirous to put her away.

4. But the angel of the Spirit appeared in this world, and after that Joseph did not put her away, but kept Mary and did not reveal this matter to any one.

5. And he did not approach Mary, but kept her as a holy virgin, though with child.

6. And he did not live with her for two months.

7. And after two months of days while Joseph was in his house, and Mary his wife, but both alone,

8. It came to pass that when they were alone that Mary straightway looked with her eyes and saw a small babe, and she was astonished.

9. And after she had been astonished, her womb was found as formerly before she had conceived.

10. And when her husband Joseph said unto her: 'What has astonished thee?' his eyes were opened, and he saw the infant and praised God, because into his portion God had come.

11. And a voice came to them: 'Tell this vision to no one.'

12. And the story regarding the infant was noised abroad in Bethlehem.

13. Some said: 'The Virgin Mary hath borne a child, before she was married two months.'

14. And many said: 'She has not borne a child, nor has a midwife gone up to her nor have we heard the cries of labour. And they were all blinded respecting Him, but they all knew regarding Him, though they knew not whence He was.

15. And they took Him, and went to Nazareth in Galilee.

16. And I saw, O Hezekiah and Josab my son, and I declare to the other prophets also who are standing by, that this hath escaped all the heavens and all the princes and all the gods of this world.

17. And I beheld that in Nazareth He sucked the breast as a babe and as is customary in order that He might not be recognized.
18. And when He had grown up He worked great signs and wonders in the land of Israel and of Jerusalem.
19. And after this the adversary envied Him and roused the children of Israel against Him, they not knowing who He was, and they delivered Him to the king, and crucified Him, and He descended to the angel of spirit prison.
20. In Jerusalem indeed I saw Him being crucified on a tree.
21. And likewise after the third day rise again and remain days.
22. And the angel who conducted me said: 'Understand, Isaiah': and I saw when He sent out the Twelve Apostles and ascended.
23. And I saw Him, and He was in the firmament, but He had not changed Himself into their form, and all the angels of the firmament saw Him and they worshipped.
24. And they said: 'How did our Lord descend in our midst, and we perceived not the glory which we see has been upon Him from the sixth heaven?'
25. And He ascended into the second heaven, and He did not transform Himself,
26. But all the angels who were on the right and on the left and the throne in the midst both worshipped Him and praised Him and said: 'How did our Lord escape us whilst descending, and we perceived not?'
27. And in like manner He ascended into the third heaven, and they praised and said in like manner.
28. And in the fourth heaven and in the fifth also they said precisely after the same manner.
29. But there was one glory, and from it He did not change Himself.
30. And I saw when He ascended into the sixth heaven, and they worshipped and glorified Him.
31. But in all the heavens the praise increased.
32. And I saw how He ascended into the seventh heaven, and all the righteous and all the angels praised Him. And then I saw Him sit down on the right hand of that Great Glory.
33. And also the angel of the Holy Spirit I saw sitting on the left hand.
34. And this angel said unto me: 'Isaiah, son of Amoz, I seal thee

up; for thou hast seen what no child of flesh, has seen.

35. And thou wilt return into thy garment of the flesh until the days are completed. Then thou wilt come hither.'

36. These things Isaiah saw and told unto all that stood before him, and they praised. And he spake to Hezekiah the King and said: 'I have spoken these things.'

37. Both the end of this world;

38. And all this vision will be consummated in the last generations.

39. And Isaiah made him swear that he would not tell it to the people of Israel, nor give these words to any man to transcribe.

40. And then ye will read. And watch ye in the Holy Spirit in order that ye may receive your garments and thrones and crowns of glory which are laid up in the seventh heaven.

41. On account of these visions and prophecies the adversary, Satan, sawed in sunder Isaiah the son of Amoz, the prophet, by the hand of Manasseh.

42. And all these things Hezekiah delivered to Manasseh in the twenty-sixth year.

43. But Manasseh did not remember them nor place these things in his heart, but becoming the servant of Satan he was destroyed. Here endeth the vision of Isaiah the prophet with his ascension.

Bibliography

Adams, Larry L. "A Statistical Style Analysis of the Book of Isaiah in Relation to the Isaiah Problem." Ph.D. dissertation, Brigham Young University, 1972.

Adams, L. La Mar, and Rencher, Alvin C. "A Computer Analysis of Isaiah Authorship Problem." *BYU Studies*, Autumn 1974, pp. 94-102.

_____. "The Popular Critical View of the Isaiah Problem in Light of Statistical Style Analysis." *Computer Studies in the Humanities and Verbal Behavior,* IV-3/4 (1973), pp. 149-57.

Buttrick, George A. et al., eds. *The Interpreter's Bible 5.* New York: Abingdon Press, 1956.

Charles, R. H., trans. The Ascension of Isaiah. London: Adam and Charles Black, 1900.

Cheyne, Thomas K. *The Prophecies of Isaiah.* New York: Thomas Whittaker, 1892.

Corbett, Don C. *Mary Fielding Smith.* Salt Lake City: Deseret Book Company, 1974.

Epstein, Isadore, ed. and trans. *The Babylonian Talmud, Nezekin, Sanhedrin.* 17 vols. London: Soncino Press, 1948.

Fohrer, Georg. *Introduction to the Old Testament.* New York: Abingdon Press, 1967.

Gottwald, Norman K. *A Light to the Nations: An Introduction to the Old Testament.* New York: Harper, 1959.

Harrison, R. K. *Introduction to the Old Testament.* Grand Rapids: William B. Eerdmans Publishing Co., 1969.

Heyerdahl, Thor. *American Indians in the Pacific.* Stockholm: Victor Pettersons Bokindustrialstielbolag, 1952.

Horn, Siegfried H. *Seventh-Day Adventist Bible Dictionary.* Washington, D. C.: Review and Herald Publishing Association, 1960, pp. 509-10.

Kimball, Spencer W. *The Miracle of Forgiveness.* Salt Lake City: Bookcraft, 1969.

McConkie, Bruce R. "Ten Keys to Understanding Isaiah." *Ensign,* Oct. 1973, pp. 78-83.

_____. *Mormon Doctrine.* 2nd ed. Salt Lake City: Bookcraft,

1966.

McKenzie, John L. *Dictionary of the Bible*. Milwaukee: The Bruce Publishing Company, 1965.

Morton, A. Q., and McLeman, James. *Paul, the Man and the Myth*. New York: Harper and Row, 1966.

Nagelsback, Carl. *The Prophet Isaiah*. New York: C. Scribner's Sons, c. 1878.

Radday, Yehuda T. "Isaiah and the Computer: A Preliminary Report." *Computers and the Humanities,* Nov. 1970, pp. 65-66.

————. "Two Computerized Statistical-Linguistic Tests Concerning the Unity of Isaiah." *Journal of Biblical Literature*, Sept. 1970, p. 324.

Robinson, George L. *The Book of Isaiah*. rev. ed. Grand Rapids: Baker Book House, 1954.

Rosenbloom, Joseph R. *The Dead Sea Isaiah Scroll, A Literary Analysis*. Grand Rapids: Eerdman's, 1970.

Smith, Joseph. *History of The Church of Jesus Christ of Latter-day Saints*. 7 vols. 2nd rev. Edited by B. H. Roberts. Salt Lake City: The Church of Jesus Christ of Latter-day Saints, 1932-51.

————. *Lectures on Faith*. Compiled by N. B. Lundwall. Salt Lake City: N. B. Lundwall, n. d.

————. *Teachings of the Prophet Joseph Smith*. Selected by Joseph Fielding Smith. Salt Lake City: Deseret Book Company, 1938.

Smith, Joseph Fielding. *Doctrines of Salvation*. 3 vols. Compiled by Bruce R. McConkie. Salt Lake City: Bookcraft, 1954-56.

Smith, Lucy Mack. *History of Joseph Smith*. Edited by Preston Nibley. Salt Lake City: Stevens & Wallis, Inc., 1945.

Sperry, Sidney B. *The Voice of Israel's Prophet*. Salt Lake City: Deseret Book Company, 1961.

Talmage, James E. *Jesus the Christ*. 3rd ed. Salt Lake City: The Church of Jesus Christ of Latter-day Saints, 1916.

Unger, Merrill F. *Introductory Guide to the Old Testament*. Grand Rapids: Zondervan Publishing, c. 1951.

Young, Edward J. *An Introduction to the Old Testament*. Grand Rapids: William B. Eerdman's Publishing Co., 1949.

Index